FOR THEIR TRIUMPHS
& FOR THEIR TEARS
WOMEN IN APARTHEID SOUTH AFRICA

HILDA BERNSTEIN

Remember all our women in the jail
Remember all our women in campaigns
Remember all our women over many fighting years
Remember all our women for their triumphs, and for their tears
(from 'Women's Day Song')

International Defence and Aid Fund for Southern Africa
Revised and enlarged edition, London, March 1985

© INTERNATIONAL DEFENCE AND AID FUND

First published 1975
Revised edition 1978
Revised and enlarged edition 1985

The production of this revised and enlarged edition was partly funded by the Women's Division of the General Board of Global Ministries, United Methodist Church, New York.

All photographs are from the photo library of IDAF Research Information and Publications Department. Cover photo by Aarhus/Fröshaug.

The International Defence and Aid Fund for Southern Africa is a humanitarian organisation which has worked consistently for peaceful and constructive solutions to the problems created by racial oppression in Southern Africa.

It sprang from Christian and humanist opposition to the evils and injustices of apartheid in South Africa. It is dedicated to the achievement of free, democratic, non-racial societies throughout Southern Africa.

The objects of the Fund are:–

  (i)   to aid, defend and rehabilitate the victims of unjust legislation and oppressive and arbitrary procedures,

 (ii)   to support their families and dependents,

(iii)   to keep the conscience of the world alive to the issues at stake.

In accordance with these three objects, the Fund distributes its humanitarian aid to the victims of racial injustice without any discrimination on grounds of race, colour, religious or political affiliation. The only criterion is that of genuine need.

The Fund runs a comprehensive information service on affairs in Southern Africa. This includes visual documentation. It produces a regular news bulletin 'FOCUS' on Political Repression in Southern Africa, and publishes pamphlets and books on all aspects of life in Southern Africa.

The Fund prides itself on the strict accuracy of all its information.

ISBN No. 0 904759 58 X

Contents

Preface 5

Introduction — Women Under Apartheid 7

Part I — Migrant Labour and Segregation 12
    I.1   Migrant labour 12
    I.2   Influx control 16
    I.3   Forced removals 21
    I.4   In the bantustans 27

Part II — Health, Welfare and the Family 35
    II.1   Marriage and the family 35
    II.2   Children 45
    II.3   Social security 46
    II.4   Control of fertility — or populations 48
    II.5   Rape 52
    II.6   Health and poverty in the countryside 53

Part III — At Work 58
    III.1   Overview 58
    III.2   Agricultural labour 59
    III.3   Domestic work 62
    III.4   Manufacturing industry 68
    III.5   Border industries 70
    III.6   The informal sector 71
    III.7   Professions 73
    III.8   Trends and patterns of discrimination 75
    III.9   Trade unions 78

Part IV — Political Struggle 81
    IV.1   A history of struggle 81
    IV.2   Women's resistance 85
    IV.3   Boycotts 94
    IV.4   A legacy of hope and defiance 96
    IV.5   The struggle continues 98
    IV.6   Soweto and after 102

Part V — Looking Forward 114

Tables 119

Appendix — Key Terms and Institutions of Apartheid 124

Pictures .... Following 128

References 129

Index 134

Preface

This book is about women in South Africa and the circumstances of their lives. It is about the social conditions and the laws that affect them, both in those areas concerned with personal, sexual and marriage relations, with children and property, and in the wider field of education and conditions of work. It is also about the ways in which women have organised in the past and are fighting today to overcome the disabilities and difficulties under which they live. It is about the part they play in the struggle for the liberation of the people of South Africa.

Earlier versions of this book were published in 1975 and 1980, and it was intended that this would be a revised and up-dated version of those editions. However, two important factors compelled a change in both the structure and the contents with the result that while this book incorporates some of the information in the earlier editions — such as those legal conditions affecting women that have not changed, and some of the historical material — the book has been substantially rewritten.

The first factor is that certain changes have taken place in South Africa in the past decade — they encompass legal, social and economic conditions and embrace the lives of people in all layers of society, and thus the lives of women in towns, in rural areas, in homes, schools and workplaces. While the fundamental structures of apartheid remain intact, some of these changes have altered the specific conditions of women's lives in important areas, and also called forth differing responses from the women. The nature of these developments is dealt with more fully in other publications, and it is the impact on women that concerns us here.

The second factor is that in the past few years, partly as a result of the increased organisation and militancy of women, there has been a growing body of research in South Africa into women's lives. There has been both a recovering of historical material, and an uncovering of contemporary conditions. Much information is now available that was not known and therefore not incorporated in the earlier versions of this book.

This book is like the opening of a front door to a house that has many rooms. What is contained here arises out of the specific South African conditions; but while apartheid is a unique system, the struggle of the women in South Africa has great significance for women in many different countries. The book shows the extent of women's opposition to the laws of apartheid, as well as to their own specific oppression that may come from historical and cultural conditions not arising directly from

5

apartheid. Superficially the situation is a contradictory one: the extent of the oppression of women, legally, socially, in every way, can scarcely be over-emphasised; they are half the population, and of that half the black majority is bound by the most extreme and harsh conditions. Yet at the same time these most oppressed women reveal the capacity for defiance, a great power of endurance, abilities to survive and protect their families, to fight oppression with ever-increasing strength and consistency.

It is the aim of this book to document the struggle of women under apartheid in South Africa. Inevitably, under the repressive conditions that exist in that country, much of the struggle is and must remain invisible and goes beyond what is recorded here.

Because apartheid is a unique system of society, without an equivalent anywhere else in the world, and because it directly affects the situation of women, it is necessary to set out briefly the most fundamental and outstanding features of this society in order to understand the legal and social position of women and the forms of their resistance. These laws are dealt with in Part I, which encompasses an explanation of migrant labour and segregation, the large-scale uprooting and removal of populations that has affected the lives of millions, and the resulting conditions in the bantustans. More detailed information on the laws and subsequent conditions may be obtained from other publications by the International Defence and Aid Fund; the concern here is to set the framework within which women's lives are enacted.

Part II deals with the family and related concerns, with the laws controlling marriage, social security and welfare, and those affecting the lives of children and the health of women and children. Some of this has been incorporated from the earlier edition, but the section on contraception, abortion and rape is entirely new, as this information has only become available fairly recently.

In Part III the changes of recent years reveal their impact upon women in relation to their work. This section covers women in all their various occupations, in industry, domestic service, agriculture, and the professions. It also describes the role of women in trade unions.

The role played by women of South Africa in the political struggle is described in Part IV. It deals with the historical background and with more contemporary events. It covers both those areas in which women, through their own organisations, mounted campaigns as women, and the campaigns of organisations embracing both men and women, in which the participation of women was vital. It also discusses the position of women within such organisations in relation to men, and in the light of feminist ideas that occupy women in many parts of the world today.

An Appendix contains an explanation of some of the institutions and terms of apartheid. For those not familiar with the apartheid system, a reading of the Appendix will make the book easier to understand.

Introduction — Women under Apartheid

South African women live in a society split by the cleavages of apartheid. The system divides the people of South Africa into separate groups, and from the enforced divisions arise differences in the position of women. It is necessary, therefore, to differentiate in describing their conditions and their lives.

The whites are a powerful and privileged minority. In spite of a considerable linguistic and cultural variety amongst them, under apartheid they form a single group in contrast to the black majority which is divided into several groups in order to facilitate the maintenance of the apartheid system and white domination.

Life roles are laid down at birth, in the first place by skin colour, in the second place by sex and economic class. To an overwhelming extent the child's whole life, her education, her possibility of achievement, jobs and status, as well as everything affecting her personal relations, is predetermined by these three factors. If the child questions the role into which she has been cast, then she will find there is no way of changing it save by changing the whole society. This applies to men as well as women, but it applies most forcibly to African women. Sexual and racial discrimination condemn them to the bottom of the pile; on their backs rests a vast superstructure of law and of custom, in which the habits and institutions of an old, pastoral society are cemented into a modern industrialised state.

A crucial factor has been the impact of imperial power on an indigenous culture. Inferiority was imposed on Africans by colonialism in Africa. The black woman had the burden trebled. The first imposition, on both women and men, was the ideology of 'inferiority' ingrained and maintained by the colonists, along with the destruction of precolonial social structures, and the denigration of any culture other than that of the colonists themselves. The second imposition arises from both the traditions of the old society and the doctrines of the new — that is, the inferior status imposed on women by the relationships between women and men. The third is that from the beginning of the development of industrialisation, sexual discrimination was embedded in the overall system of exploitation.

The black majority of South Africa was divided into separate groups by the colonial powers, and is still divided today by apartheid. Each group is administered in different ways, reflecting the differences in the conditions and origins of their oppression. The principal divisions of the black population (explained more fully in the Appendix) are referred to here as 'African', 'Indian' and 'Coloured' *(see Table I)*. Within each group, the position of women is generally even worse than that of men.

The factors that most strongly control women's lives are embedded in the apartheid system. Apartheid divides people into separate groups where class and colour tend to coincide. Different laws apply to the separate groups and their living conditions differ widely. Therefore the descriptions and explanations of these must also be separated although there are some areas where the problems and disabilities arising from sexual discrimination overlay those deriving from racial discrimination. But generally speaking, the majority of South African women suffer first and foremost from the effects of apartheid. Since an awareness of what apartheid is and how it operates is essential for understanding the position of women in South Africa, the briefest outline follows.

The stratification of South African society has its basis in colonial conquest. The consolidation of domination by the white minority, and the perpetuation of racial laws and ways of thinking, has been basic to the policies of successive governments.

The economic foundations of the modern industrial economy in South Africa were laid down with the establishment of large-scale gold and diamond mining in the nineteenth century. The economy of the region, until then predominantly agricultural, underwent rapid industrialisation, based on a supply of cheap labour secured largely through control of the land by the white minority.

The process by which the mass of the people who occupied the land were dispossessed and excluded from access to it has been a long and continuous one. They were driven off the land by force of arms in most of the country over a period of over two centuries; by the imposition of taxes which could not be paid without a cash income — which in turn could only be obtained by participating in the settler economy; and by other administrative means.

The scale of the dispossession has been enormous. It is reflected in laws which together designated 13.7 per cent of the whole country for Africans, and the rest, nearly 87 per cent, for the white minority (apart from a very small amount designated to black people other than Africans). The African areas consisted of fragments scattered throughout the country, and these, the 'reserves', have today become the basis of the bantustan system.

The second outstanding feature of South Africa's industrialisation was the utilisation of migrant labour, originally almost entirely male, controlled by the pass law system. The vast majority of African women were left outside the industrial labour market, while male migrants served a period of contract labour away from their homes for most of the year, with women, children, old and disabled people subsisting on small pieces of land in the bantustans. The result has been an extreme form of exploitation of both migrants and their families. By leaving the workers' families on the land it was possible to pay lower wages and avoid having to build houses and supply those services that are essential to maintain urban populations and ensure the reproduction of the labour force. It was assumed that the women would feed their families off the produce of the land. The employer could obtain a labour supply at less than the wage necessary to maintain the worker's family, while ensuring the continued supply of labour through annual leave periods which allowed the conception of children.

From the beginning of industrialisation, therefore, African women were relegated to a position which had ever-spreading disadvantages. They were to fulfil their traditional role as bearers of children; they were to work on the land to supplement the low wages of the male migrants (only now they had to perform both their own tasks and those of the absent men). And they were to be denied the gradual access to paid employment that would normally have provided them with a new status in a changing society.

The original conditions of this pattern of labour have long disappeared. For several decades the bantustans have no longer been able to support their populations, even at subsistence levels. The policies of apartheid have caused a further decline in the capacity of the bantustan areas to produce enough to feed the population there. Enforced removals of people into the bantustans led to a massive rise in their population. Black agriculture was starved of investment funds. At the same time government policies have in various ways further restricted black access to land for cultivation to an even smaller proportion of the population in the bantustans: two-thirds of that population is now landless.

The breakdown in rural life could not lead to the profound changes in social structures that would normally have followed a shift from a subsistence-based economy, because of the laws of apartheid, and because of the way in which colonial administrators perpetuated certain customs long after the type of life that gave rise to them had been lost. These customs maintained and reinforced the subjugation of women in ways described in the chapters that follow.

But the most devastating aspect of apartheid has been the programme of mass removals, the uprooting and relocation of people through forced evictions in order to achieve a territorial segregation of the population according to the policies of apartheid (see Appendix for further explanation).

9

One of the principal means by which this policy of relocating and controlling populations is enforced is the pass law system, a key instrument of apartheid and one of the main factors in the oppression of women.

It is through the operation of the pass laws and other instruments of apartheid that human beings become units to be shifted around a changing map of South Africa with total disregard for families, communities, homes, employment. In our times in different parts of the world there have been large-scale emigrations and movements of populations caused primarily by war, conflict or famine. But not since the era of the slave trade have such huge numbers of people been forcibly taken from homes and land, forcibly removed, and 'relocated', against their will. The apartheid regime may claim the unique distinction of being the only ruling power of our times which is deliberately dismembering a unified country, to separate the different strands that make up a nation long consolidated by industrial development.

The map of South Africa has been cut to pieces and reassembled to suit the ideology and economy of apartheid. The cost in mass human suffering is appalling and the divisions created will leave deep scars.

Yet in South Africa it is not the differences between groups of people that are crucial; it is the fact that regardless of all apartheid laws, they share the same country, are integrated into its industrial apparatus and cannot truly be separated without destroying the way of life that the whites wish to hold for themselves. The advance of industrialisation brought about a process of assimilation that cannot be abrogated. Under the impact of urban conditions, black and white increasingly share the same culture, a unique culture arising from the mingling of contributions from many different origins.

The strongest impulses in South African society are towards national integration. Hence the tremendous barriers of laws that apartheid must erect to divide people.

It is from this complicated range of custom and law that women's conditions must be extracted. The span of conditions is enormous, from the desolation of the bantustans where many women live in extreme poverty and near-starvation to the luxurious suburban areas of the towns where white women are encased in splendidly appointed homes.

South African women, black and white, live in a society that is not only racialist, but also deeply sexist. The racialism and sexism are intertwined. Sexism in South Africa is not only revealed in cultural attitudes, but is embedded in the legal institutions.

White women, who share the right to vote with white men, and who have access to higher education and live in physically well-endowed conditions, live also in this sexist, male-dominated society. The women are absent from the organs of decision-making and control in politics, in the economy and in the armed forces.

However, the range and potency of these disabilities vary greatly between the different 'population groups', and the system of apartheid under which they live exercises decisive control over the direction of all their lives. Despite their disadvantages relative to white men (familiar to women in many countries), most white women support or actively help to perpetuate the apartheid system which gives them privileges and benefits at the expense of the black majority. The majority of women, that is the black women and more specifically African women, suffer first and foremost because they are black. Black women's specific disabilities, whether arising from social custom, cultural indoctrination or legal barriers, cannot be separated from the overall system of apartheid.

Black women in South Africa suffer from a three-fold oppression: as blacks; as women; and as workers who largely form a reserve army of labour. The three strands are interlaced. Black women cannot change the immediate conditions of their lives without fighting against the restrictions on, for example, free movement or access to education, both of which are controlled by apartheid laws. To fight male domination they need to fight the basis on which bantustans are established, in fact to fight the whole balkanisation of their country. To maintain family life, they must enter the field as protagonists against migratory labour and the pass laws.

It is for these reasons that this book concentrates mainly on the laws, customs and situation of African women, for they are both the majority and at the same time the most oppressed women in South Africa.

I. Migrant Labour and Segregation

The structure of apartheid is built on a system of migrant labour and territorial segregation. For black people in South Africa this means strict controls on their movement, on where they may live and where they may work. For many it means a more or less permanent separation of families. It means the forced removal and relocation of population, and the destruction of many black communities. For black women, above all for African women, it means particularly intense forms of exploitation and oppression.

I.1 Migrant Labour

Many parts of the world are familiar with the phenomenon of migrant workers — 'guest-workers' — leaving their own country to work in another for a specified period. In South Africa, too, there are workers from other countries of Southern Africa. However, in South Africa migrant labour exists also primarily in a special form as an integral and basic part of the apartheid system. In the distorting mirror of apartheid, all Africans working outside the bantustans are officially considered to be migrants who leave their own 'country' to work in 'white' South Africa — a different country.

This precept is applied in varying degrees to all black workers, and not only to those from the bantustans working on temporary contract outside the bantustans.

By law all Africans must carry passes, and those who gain residence rights outside the bantustans are given them only as qualifications to the general rule which says that they are citizens of another country.

Every person, black or white has to live in an area designated as their 'own area'. For the white minority this means most of the country including the areas where almost all economic activity is based. For the black majority it means living either in a bantustan, or a white-owned farm, or in a black 'township' near a 'white' town. For many black women in domestic work it means living on the white employer's property in separate accommodation. The townships are segregated dormitory areas with virtually no commercial or industrial activity and few opportunities for employment outside what is sometimes called the informal sector. Most of those who live in the townships must, if they are employed, travel each day to work in the 'white' areas.

Since the 1960s the black townships have been concentrated into big regional townships far from town and city centres. This has often involved enforced removals of people and the destruction of existing and sometimes mixed communities which were located closer to work and other facilities.

Where it has been possible the government has created the new townships just inside the bantustan borders, close enough to centres of economic activity to allow workers to travel each day or each week to work outside the bantustans. In a special meaning that apartheid gives the word, they are described as 'commuters' (people who travel from their 'own areas' to work). Restrictions on the building of housing for Africans outside the bantustans have created a deliberate shortage of family housing, forcing ever more people to become 'squatters', to become contract labourers and live away from their families (often in single-sex hostels), or to move to the bantustan townships to become commuters. As modern transport has developed the distances have grown greater.

The full extent of migrant labour in South Africa is not known, because official figures count only those on formally registered temporary contracts to work outside their places of residence. Many others are also forced to live away from their families for the week, or the year, and travel home whenever they can (see Table II).

While almost all the foreign migrants were men in 1980, one quarter of the internal migrant workers were women.[2]

In Migrant Labour in South Africa Francis Wilson says that the migrant labour system is based on the premise that a human being can be broken into two parts: a 'labour unit' working in the town, separated from the other part, a man with a family, with hopes and aspirations. 'If man was seen primarily as a human being who among other things was a worker, then such exclusion would not be possible.'[3]

This split is most clearly seen in the division of the family imposed by migrant labour. But a divided life is imposed on all black people in South Africa. The township system is both part and an extension of the migrant labour system. Together they profoundly shape the lives of all black people in South Africa.

Nevertheless apartheid rests on migrant labour in its fullest sense, and it is the condition of those caught up most directly in this form of labour which most clearly reveals the heart of apartheid and its impact on women.

Migrant labour, as other communities have found to their cost, has an adverse effect on family life and social development, since the men and women who should be playing their part as husbands and wives, as mothers and fathers, and as members of the community are absent for long periods. Where such dislocation is temporary and small-scale the effects may be remedied but in South Africa a large section of workers are permanently migrant workers.

13

'We are trying to introduce the migratory labour pattern as far as possible in every sphere', stated a prominent Nationalist MP, Mr G F van L Froneman, who later became Deputy Minister of Justice, Mines and Planning. 'This is, in fact, the entire basis of our policy as far as the white economy is concerned.'[4]

In 1969 Mr Froneman named the conditions under which 'foreign labour' (he was referring to Africans from South Africa) could be used without conflicting with apartheid. This included the denial of rights of domicile or citizenship outside the bantustans. He emphasised that the 'African labour force must not be burdened with superfluous appendages such as wives, children and dependants who could not provide service'.[5]

'We need them to work for us,' stated the then Prime Minister, B J Vorster, in 1968 'but the fact that they work for us can never entitle them to claim political rights. Not now, nor in the future . . . under any circumstances.'[6]

---

1.   It is accepted Government policy that the Bantu* are only temporarily resident in the European areas of the Republic, for as long as they offer their labour there. As soon as they become, for some reason or another, no longer fit for work or superfluous in the labour market, they are expected to return to their country of origin or the territory of the national unit where they fit in ethnically if they were not born and bred in the homeland.

2.   The Bantu in the European areas who are normally regarded as non-productive and as such have to be resettled in the homelands, are conveniently classified as follows:–

(i) the aged, the unfit, widows with dependent children and also families who do not qualify under the provisions of the Bantu (Urban Areas) Act No. 25, of 1945 for family accommodation in the European urban areas;

(ii) Bantu on European farms who become superfluous as a result of age, disability or the application of Chapter IV of the Bantu Trust and Land Act, No. 18 of 1936, or Bantu squatters from mission stations and black spots which are being cleared up;

(iii) Professional Bantu such as doctors, attorneys, agents, traders, industrialists, etc. Also such persons are not regarded as essential for the European labour market, and as such they must also be settled in the homelands in so far as they are not essential for serving their compatriots in the European areas.

(The Secretary for Bantu Administration and Development, General Circular No. 25, 1967, quoted in 'African Population Relocation in South Africa', G. Mare, SAIRR, 1980)
*For an explanation of the apartheid term 'Bantu', see Appendix

---

14

The official term, 'temporary sojourners', is applied to African workers who are integrated with and an integral part of the country's economy. They are allowed to work in that economy because it would collapse without them. But they are not regarded as human beings. A resolution passed at the 1973 Congress of the Afrikaanse Studentebond (Afrikaner students' organisation) demanded that 'All the black women and children in the white area be shipped back to the homelands and only the men should be left in the white areas for as long as we need them.'[7]

Other aspects of the official view are no less inhuman. 'We do not want the Bantu women here simply as an adjunct to the procreative capacity of the Bantu population.'[8] A wife should be allowed into the town only if she were needed on the labour market. Her husband could visit her in the bantustans from time to time.

This official concept of family life for Africans is underlined in a circular from the Department of Bantu Administration and Development to local authorities in 1969. The circular put forward the proposition that where a (white) town is close to a 'homeland' (a bantustan), the Africans employed in that town should actually live in the 'homeland'. Should the distance between town and 'homeland' be too great, however, hostel accommodation should be provided for the workers in the urban areas, and they should be able to visit their families periodically.

When a voluntary welfare organisation wrote to all South African churches in 1974 stating that since the church preached the sanctity of marriage and family life they should protest against official policy, the largest of the Christian Churches, the Nederduits Gereformeerde Kerk (Dutch Reformed Church) replied, 'That families in many cases cannot live together is true but it is also true that they are granted the opportunity to visit each other — provided of course they are willing to comply with the relevant regulations and they do not disregard this privilege.'[9]

In spite of claims in recent years by the South African regime both internally and internationally, that apartheid is undergoing radical alteration and reform, migrant labour remains a key aspect of the system.

Women and the Migrant Labour System

Migrant labour deeply disrupts the lives of South African women. The system itself makes it virtually illegal for many African women to live with their husbands, except during the annual two-week holiday when migrant workers may go to visit their wives in the bantustans. It makes a mockery of family life, creating an impassable chasm between husband and wife.

Official statistics about the marital status of South African women of various groups tell their own story about the social consequences of the migrant labour system *(see Table III)*.

The migrant labour system affects the lives of most people living in the bantustans, a large proportion of workers outside the bantustans, and indirectly the lives of all South Africans, black and white. During the long periods of their youthful, sexually active lives, husbands and wives must live apart. For many, a family unit is never formed.

Francis Wilson sums up the evidence of his research on migrant labour with a devastating list of 31 arguments against it, including many that touch directly on the lives of women. Among others, it aggravates and creates illegitimacy, bigamy and prostitution; homosexuality and drunkenness; breakdown of parental authority; malnutrition, tuberculosis and venereal disease. Together with influx control and mass removals under 'resettlement' plans, migrant labour is depriving millions of black women of the most elementary and fundamental rights.

I.2 Influx Control

South Africa's migrant workers and their families do not freely choose to live and work under the conditions just described. A vast legal and administrative apparatus, backed up by armed force, is used to maintain the migrant labour system. The measures used to enforce these policies are called 'Influx Control', and the laws are known as the 'Pass Laws'.

The idea that families of migrants would secure their own subsistence from the land in the bantustans was based on an assumption of a static subsistence sector of the economy, untouched by industrialisation or by the introduction of commercial farming in the rest of the country. There was, however, no way of confining these changes to a single sector of the economy: they penetrated the whole society, leading to the dissolution of existing modes of production in some areas and the conservation of their forms, although in a stunted and distorted manner, in others.[11] However, the system depended on keeping as many women as possible in the 'reserves'. If the whole family becomes part of urban industrial society then the claimed rationale for setting the payment of the male worker at the level of a single man falls away. Thus African women were until recently denied access to the new skills and the new relationships of developing capitalism except in insignificant numbers. When they did become wage-earners it was mainly in domestic service and agriculture, where they were not part of an organised labour force.

Subsistence production underwent constant change. It became almost exclusively the concern of women, doubling their work-load. This was coupled with a decline in the productivity of the land, starting in the 1920s, that has gradually reduced material conditions until a large proportion of women and their dependants in the bantustans are undernourished and underclothed, dependent for survival on the remittance

16

from the male migrant. This is illustrated by research published in 1975 which showed that at a time when the minimum needed to sustain families in what was described as 'human poverty' was said to be R103.99 per month, families in the Nqutu area of Natal, part of the KwaZulu bantustan, barely subsisted on R14.87 per month. A study carried out in 1981 in the Mahlabatini area in the same region, concluded cautiously that the average household income in the community of eight thousand people was 'well below a fairly widely used poverty measure.' More tellingly still, the study showed that those in the area, of whom 92 per cent were women and children, were heavily dependent for survival, even at this inadequate level, on remittances from migrant workers. For a household of eight, the average in the area, the Household Subsistence Level would have been R184 per month in that area. The average household income, from all sources, was in fact only R114. Income from subsistence production was a mere R38. The bulk of household income was made up of remittances from migrant workers (R50) and pensions (R18), with a smaller amount from local employment (R5.50), home enterprise (R5) and agricultural sales (R4). Yet another study in a third area showed that in 1984 entire rural families were 'severely malnourished and on the verge of collapse' in parts of the KwaZulu bantustan as a result of the retrenchment of migrant workers.[12]

The only way of trying to make women and their families remain in such conditions was to make it difficult for them to move to the urban areas (to seek work, join the men, find food for their children). Thus the pass laws were extended to women in the 1950s.[13]

Every African over 16 years old outside the bantustan areas must carry a pass book; these are a form of identification that records where the holder may live, where he or she is employed, whether taxes have been paid, and other vital information for total control.

For women from the bantustans the pass book contains a section for the consent of the commissioner of the district defined as home, and for the consent of father, male guardian or husband to her going to work or live in another district.

Pass books have to be produced at all points of contact with officials and can be used to control every aspect of life. The pass laws bear even more heavily on African women than on African men. Not only do they need this male consent to leave home or to work in another place, but since 1964 a total ban was placed on the further entry of women into the urban areas outside the bantustans except on a visitor's permit.

Pass laws of one kind or another have applied to African men since the nineteenth century and even earlier in some parts of what is now South Africa.

African women remained outside the pass laws framework until 1952 and their struggle against the pass laws, beginning in 1913, is an epic

17

story, related in Part IV. Before the 1950s, African women did not have to carry passes. Nevertheless, it was still more difficult for women than for men to move to the expanding towns, largely because of employment practices and restrictions on the provision of family housing. In most areas of work employers recruited mainly men, and in some areas exclusively men.

Whenever substantial numbers of African women have been drawn into wage labour, moves have been made to extend influx control to them. The first attempt, in 1913, was unsuccessful. But with changing patterns of industrialisation and with the progressive deterioration of subsistence agriculture under the impact of apartheid, the number of women in wage labour increased rapidly. This was particularly marked during the 1940s when manufacturing industry expanded. In 1952 the whole system of influx control was reviewed and streamlined. The changes included the extension to African women of the requirement to carry passes. As a result African women could only come to the towns and cities to seek work with the permission of rural labour bureaux. They could however still come as dependants of men who were resident in town. In 1964 this right was withdrawn. Women already in employment and those who already had rights of residence could stay, but others could come to the towns only as contract workers. Those who came on any other basis did so illegally. In 1968 all building of family accommodation in the urban areas was stopped.

Occasionally loopholes have been opened by taking issues to court: but they have been relatively minor or quickly closed. The legal victories, though small and precarious, have been important. At the same time they underline the fact that unless they have been born in an urban area outside a bantustan, most African women are dependent on their relationship to men for residence rights.[14]

A court ruling in 1964 established that African women could not be legally prevented from entering urban areas outside the bantustans ('prescribed' areas), but only from remaining there more than 72 hours without permission. In 1980 another ruling established the rights of wives and children to live in 'prescribed' areas with their husbands or fathers, if the men themselves qualified under the pass laws to remain there. When a court ruled in 1983 that contract workers could gain rights of permanent residence after ten years working for the same employer, the way seemed open for many families divided by the migrant labour system to be united and for many others living together 'illegally' to do so openly. However within months the law was amended in a way that effectively nullified these rulings except in the case of a few people. Only those who lived in 'approved' accommodation could benefit from the rulings, and there was no right for people who met the other conditions to demand such accommodation.

18

The control which the authorities have over housing is one of the most powerful weapons in the armoury of influx control.

Controls Strengthened

The nature of South Africa's system for the control and direction of African labour was the subject of an official commission of inquiry, the Riekert Commission, appointed in the wake of the uprisings of 1976 at a time when the existing controls were conspicuously failing. The policies emanating from this commission, described in more detail in the next section, rested on two fundamental premises. On the one hand the permanence of a section of African people in urban areas outside the bantustans was to be recognised in law and administrative practice. They would have residence rights and preferential access to jobs and housing. On the other hand, any other Africans would be admitted to those areas only if, and for as long as, their labour was required and if there was housing for them. These measures were aimed at making the influx control system more efficient. They represented 'a change in mechanism, not in policy', the Prime Minister informed Parliament in 1980.[15]

The consequence of these policies, still being implemented in practice, is the drawing of a line between a minority of 'insiders', who draw some benefit from the change, and the majority, the 'outsiders', for whom the change means an intensification of the controls which keep them in the bantustans or on the white-owned farms unless their labour is needed elsewhere.

Even the 'insiders' remain non-citizens in the areas where they are recognised as 'permanently' living, obliged to live in the segregated townships, with no political rights beyond the local level except through the bantustans. In many respects their situation differs little from that of the third category which has come into existence as a direct result of government policy and is destined to become perhaps the largest group of all if the government succeeds in its intentions. These are the commuters, who spend the day, or the week, in the 'white' areas working and at night or at weekends stay in the bantustan townships spread around the edges of the great industrial and commercial areas of the country.

The changes have borne heavily on women. The earlier restrictions had made it difficult, and illegal, for African women to live in an urban area outside bantustans, but many defied the obstacles. The new measures, shifting much of the work of implementing influx control from the police to employers and those who provide accommodation, have magnified the difficulties. The controls have become more effective.

Employers who previously employed 'illegals' are now deterred by the large fines they would have to pay if discovered. The fines were increased in 1979 to R500 per 'illegal' employee. Just before the increased fines were applied, the government announced a 'moratorium' to allow employers of 'illegals' to legalise the situation: instead of the employers being fined their employees were registered as contract workers, that is with the right to remain only until the expiry of a one-year contract which would not be automatically renewed. The many African women illegally in these areas were relegated to near-permanent unemployment.[16]

The introduction of the new policies of influx control since 1979 saw increased arrests under the pass laws, increased destruction by the authorities of unofficial 'unapproved' accommodation, increased removals under the pass laws to the bantustans.

This period was also one in which there was a dramatic increase in the number of African women in wage labour. This was in part a result of changing patterns of industrialisation, but also a response to falling living standards for black families, brought about by recession and inflation and, fundamentally, the deepening poverty in bantustans overcrowded by apartheid policies.[17] In 1983, with conditions in rural areas made even worse by a prolonged drought, it was estimated that 85,000 people, a large proportion of them women, were moving each month to the towns and cities — part of what was described as 'an irreversible flow that will see another twenty million blacks cram urban areas over the next 20 years . . . The trend will continue despite Government efforts to bulldoze "squatter camps" and their shanty towns back into the distant veld.'[18] *(See Table IV).*

When the police arrested me in 1982, I was given no choice of what to do with my children (aged two and four). Both were vomiting and had diarrhoea. I was allowed to take them to the prison hospital where I saw a nurse who gave them medicine but it was not right for their problem. I saw no doctor. There were about 30 to 40 of us in a cell. We slept on the mat on the cold cement floor as there were no beds. When I was busy I would tie my baby on my back and the older one would just stand next to me. Neither we nor the children ever went outside for exercise. There were no toys or books . . . and no supervision. I was given no change of clothing for myself or the children, apart from one napkin. We were given no special food for the babies. The children received the same food as us. In the morning we had mealie meal, skim milk, a little bread and black coffee with no sugar. At lunch time we ate mealie rice with a little meat. We had vegetables once a week and no fruit at all. In the evenings we had porridge, mealie meal, coffee and a slice of bread sometimes spread with fat.

(A mother arrested under the pass laws who spent five weeks in prison in 1981 and four in 1982, both times with two of her children: during 1984 3,415 children were imprisoned with their mothers — Argus 20.12.84)

I.3 Forced Removals

The Uprooting of Millions

More than three and a half million people have been forcibly moved in South Africa since 1960, most of them Africans. At least another 1.7 million people were still under threat of removal in 1984. Many people have been moved more than once and others live in fear of further enforced removal.[20]

The true dimensions of the uprooting of South Africans are difficult to estimate. The government does not encourage accurate assessments. The Laws on Co-operation and Development Act of 1982 provides for information related to removals to be kept secret, making it even more difficult to obtain details.

The mass removal of population takes various forms (as explained in the Appendix). In rural areas tenants have been evicted from white-owned farms and communities forced off land which had been theirs for generations. In towns and cities existing black residential areas have been destroyed and their residents moved into larger, more sharply segregated, townships further away from the main centres of employment, and often inside bantustan boundaries. People living in unauthorised residential areas (the homes of so-called 'squatter' communities) established in towns and cities in defiance of influx control are under almost constant attack and threat of removal to bantustans.

We have lived here for 40 years. I have seven children and I am a widow. My sister's eight children also live with us because they have nowhere else to live. I work in Pinetown as a domestic servant and earn R50 a month. They have now thrown me out of my mother's house and expect us all to live in a four-roomed house in the township.

When they moved us they did not say how much they would pay us. There were 17 mango trees in bloom, in addition to guavas, sugar cane, avocado pears, oranges and bananas on the land from which we have been evicted. Over the years I sold fruit to help buy clothes and food for the family. Now it's all gone.

(A woman speaking in 1981 about being forced from her home — Daily News, 23.8.81)

The financial costs of the programme of forced removals have been astronomical.[21] But the cost in terms of the destruction of communities, of alienation, the loss of stability, the undermining of rural black society and human suffering, degradation and humiliation cannot be counted.[22] It is a modern tragedy on a vast scale, in which the pursuit of hard profits adorned with an ideology that enjoys the support of a small proportion of

21

the population is creating a disaster encompassing the lives and futures of millions of people. Protests, petitions, resistance to removals, pleas, deputations — nothing produces even the faintest glimmering of human compassion.

'Relocation, for whatever reason, is a violent and brutal process', writes a contemporary historian, Joanne Yawitch. She describes how it leads to a deterioration in material conditions and impoverishment and how the trauma and insecurity of resettlement have severe effects on personal relations. The creation of division and hostility, even within some families, she says, is an inevitable effect of forced removals.

These are not simply side-effects of removal, but integral to it. In other words, removal of people is not simply a physical act; it is part of a process and a strategy that seeks to push increasing numbers of South Africa's people into ever more remote and inhospitable areas where, broken and fragmented by the experience of removal and all that it means, people are left to exist under conditions of increasing apathy and power-lessness.[23]

Sada, a typical relocation camp, was established in 1976 in the Ciskei. Thirty thousand people were crammed into this area, living in two-roomed houses, each room approximately two square metres in area. Adjacent to Sada was a mud village, nicknamed 'Village of Tears', populated by people unable to cram into Sada. Facilities for its estimated ten thousand people were virtually non-existent. There were 13 toilets — privately-owned; the rest of the population had to make do with the bush. There was not a single tap in the village, and people had to go to the neighbouring Sada for water.[24]

Effects on Women

Life in these areas bears no resemblance to that lived formerly on the land. The effects on women are particularly severe.

Winterveld is only 15 kilometres from the administrative capital of South Africa, Pretoria, but it is within the area designated as the Bophuthatswana bantustan. Because it is near a city that provides a certain amount of work, from the 1960s large numbers of squatters moved there renting land on which to build shacks. Its current population is estimated at three-quarters of a million or more. The resulting effects on the lives of the women have been investigated and analysed by Joanne Yawitch, and these are some of her findings.

For the majority of women there is no work; they are dependent on the wages of husbands, mostly unskilled workers. They must accept whatever they can get, however little, without question. 'In Winterveld it is common to find women who starve themselves to feed their husbands and children because there is so little money . . . Women tell with extreme bitterness that they do not know how much their husbands earn.'

This is the first factor in their powerlessness. Then the men themselves work under conditions of exploitation which, because of their lack of political power and their exclusion from collective bargaining, are often beyond their control. 'It is the women who bear the brunt of the frustration and aggression that their husbands are powerless to express within the workplace. In Winterveld wife and child-beating is as common as rape. Sexual aggression is, in a situation such as this, a more or less immutable fact of life.' Yawitch goes on to explain that the isolation that defines the lives of 'housewives' in many Western countries is, in this situation, total.

Forced removal and resettlement lead not only to breakdown within the family. The community organisations and their essential work are also destroyed. Unity and co-operation can only grow where there is some security. Women are strongly drawn to community groups, often church-based, called *manyanos*, and organise associations called *stockfels*, a form of mutual saving and financial support. With the removals, the *manyanos* and *stockfels* disappear, their basis of neighbourly friendship and co-operation having been destroyed.

Forced removal and resettlement play a major role in suppressing organised opposition to apartheid policies through this destruction of stable communities and social structures, and the placing together of a haphazard assortment of people, often strangers, who in the harsh struggle for individual survival cannot form new relationships. Often this is compounded by the fact that many people have been moved more than once, often three or four times.

So we went to Taaibosch farm (in the Oranje-Vaal administration area) in 1946.

We lived on that farm in a shack that we built ourselves. Then the mother of my mother died in 1956. I was married there, and I had three of my four children on that farm. My elder daughter also married on the farm and had two daughters there.

But Mrs Koller died in August last year, and her son took over the farm. He told my mother she had to be out in November last year because she was too old to do the work, and when she told him that she had nowhere to go he said he could not build proper houses for his employees and she must go.

I do not know what to do. The police have come and said they will knock down our house if we do not go before the end of this month.

(A woman speaking in 1981 about life as a farm worker — Star 31.1.81)

23

More than community relations is destroyed when the communities are uprooted, scattered, and relocated in barren and hostile places. Relocation obliterates tradition, continuity, culture, history. Often people have lived in the places from which they are removed for generations; their multiple interlocking relationships are destroyed. Relocation obliterates homes, possessions, smallholdings, gardens (they all gave valuable access to growing food). It obliterates schools, churches, clinics. It obliterates communities.

Resistance and Defiance

In spite of its power, and even though community after community has been uprooted, the regime frequently encounters tenacious and courageous resistance on the part of those it wishes to remove by force.

The name 'Crossroads' has come to symbolise the resistance of women to forced removals. It is a defiant assertion of determination to establish the right to live with their husbands and to have a family life.

The government decided in 1954 to remove African workers from the Western Cape and to declare the area a 'Coloured Labour Preference Area'. Over the years, thousands of Africans were shifted out of the Western Cape to the bantustans, where necessity drove them back again to the Western Cape, now not in family groups, but as migrant or contract workers. At the same time, building of family housing for Africans was stopped (in 1955) with a resulting acute shortage of accommodation.

Male workers were permitted to enter Cape Town, but forced to live in single-sex compounds or hostels. The women, with their children, returned to the Cape. Outside the officially designated areas, they erected shelters, built homes and established communities. Lacking official permission to do so, they were regarded as 'squatters'. Crossroads was one of several squatters' camps that grew on wasteland and in the bush surrounding the city.

Among the first squatters to be removed were those of Modderdam, with a population of ten thousand, in the Western Cape. An official notice in July 1977 told them: 'You are hearby advised of my intention to demolish buildings or structures and to remove material from the land . . . mechanical equipment will be used to demolish buildings and structures and closed or locked buildings will be summarily demolished . . .' The demolition of three thousand dwellings was completed in five days. Women and children remained guarding their possessions in the open while the men went to work. The government claimed that many evicted squatters had accepted rail tickets to their 'homeland', the Transkei, but squatters denied this, saying they had no homes to go to. Most were absorbed into other squatters' camps.

Unibel, not far from Modderdam, was a settled community of twenty thousand people with a school. Demolitions, in July 1978, took five days and a report made by the medical faculty at Cape Town University stated:

> Children aged two to three weeks spent three or four consecutive nights in the open, and there was rain on two occasions . . . There were no facilities for boiling water or milk, and following the demolition of the latrines . . . it was not possible further to separate water and faeces . . . The condition of the camp deteriorated so that the Unibel area was an area of stench, enormous numbers of flies and a fair number of stray and hungry animals.

The report concluded that the demolition was executed in total disregard for the health and well-being of every individual concerned, in the most inhumane manner.[25]

Soon after the destruction and removal of the communities at Modderdam and Unibel, the government moved against the people at Crossroads, also in the Western Cape, encountering more organised and sustained resistance, described below.

Although camps like Unibel and Modderdam were demolished by the authorities, in Crossroads, with community resistance, and backed by public support and legal assistance from white sympathisers, the attacks were held off. The Women's Committee at Crossroads was particularly strong and active. The women kept watch to prevent the surreptitious demolition of homes. They sat down before bulldozers and refused to move. They dramatised their struggle in theatre, and took it to other parts of the country. It was also projected on television in Europe and the United States.

The women graphically described the grinding poverty and hardship behind their defiance of the authorities in leaving the bantustans and living in squatter camps.

Now Crossroads is to be eliminated, and the people are being moved to Khayelitsha, a vast, windswept area of sand-dunes and bush. George Morrison, Deputy Minister of Co-operation and Development, recognised what the resistance of the women of Crossroads has meant when he stated that Crossroads was 'a symbol of provocation and blackmail of the government and we want to destroy that symbol at all costs'.[26]

The episodes and stories cannot be encompassed within this book. But what happened to another group of squatters at Nyanga Township tells a little of the incredible cruelty and hardship that the women are forced to endure.

This was in August of 1981. Cape Town police swooped on 1,500 squatters and loaded them on to buses and trains for a 600-mile journey to what they called their 'homeland' — the Transkei. A thousand women and children went by bus and then train to Umtata, the principal town of the Transkei, and were disgorged in teeming rain on to the main street, from whence they sought shelter in churches. Hundreds more were put on other buses to travel even further away. It all happened so quickly that mothers were separated from children — one mother left behind a baby who was in hospital in Cape Town, and whom she had been breast-feeding.

Desperate to reunite their families and retrieve their possessions, the women began to try to filter back to Cape Town. A white church worker, Kathy Luckett, accompanied 54 of these women to the end of their journey, when the ones who got through — 15 of them — exhausted, straggled into Cape Town. At Queenstown, Kathy Luckett saw 'long queues of blanketed figures huddled together in the hail at a road block', and at Cradock, in the pouring rain, imploring hands stretched out, confused faces 'and endless last-minute messages'.

The razing of the Nyanga squatters' camp by armed policemen with dogs on a bitterly cold winter dawn was described by a journalist as a desperate act to turn the tide of the ever-increasing African urban population.[27] Against all odds, despite the demolition of their shanties, the destruction of their possessions, in defiance of the armed police, the vicious dogs, the night-time raids, the women, by their unrelenting persistence, fought back. The unyielding determination of the women to maintain their families at all costs is shown by the story of the bed-people, whose beds became their homes as the authorities confiscated and destroyed all plastic and other covers erected around them. The bed-people tore down their shacks every dawn, burying branches and plastic sheets in the sand, and leaving the beds unprotected during a bitter Cape winter. Their presence was in itself a political statement and a challenge to apartheid. Thus such camps are not simply an expression of their compelling needs. They are also a challenge to the system of migratory labour.

In her study on women and squatting, Joanne Yawitch writes that African women 'occupy a pivotal position within apartheid's repressive system of labour control. As long as they can be kept out of the urban areas, or as long as they are there only as migrant domestic workers, the foundations of the system still stand secure.'

She goes on to say that it is in this sense that one must understand the nature of the challenge posed by the women who refuse to rot in the bantustans, and form squatters' camps outside the towns where the male migrant workers are employed and where women have some hope of seeking work. 'In choosing to live together as families, they are challenging the basis of the entire cheap labour power in South Africa.'

She concludes that the conflicts that arise between women and men are rooted in the migrant labour system, and that an overall improvement for both women and men rests primarily on the abolition of migrant labour with its pass laws and other means of control.[28]

The status of women can only undergo a fundamental change in South Africa when the migrant labour system is abolished and when women are able to take part on equal terms in the economic life of their country.

I.4 In the Bantustans

There are over five million African women living in the bantustans. They suffer disabilities in virtually every facet of their existence, an existence to which they are bound by a complex interlacing of customary and common law, together with the fact that, unlike men, they are less able to escape by going to the cities. For two decades influx control and pass laws have prevented most African women from taking up lawful residence in the cities and the urban areas.

African women in the cities are subject to many of the same disabilities that affect the women in the bantustans; but in the latter there are some differences and added disabilities arising from the distortion by white governments of customs and laws of a former society. The insistence by the rulers of apartheid South Africa that what they call the indigenous culture must be preserved in the bantustans leads to contradictions that cannot be resolved today — any more than the clock can be turned back to restore a former type of society — and it is the women who suffer most from the anomalous situation.

Quite apart from the problems of trying to maintain traditional structures and laws in an advanced industrialised state, the government has made a parody of traditional institutions, keeping the form but removing the content.

The retention of the system of chiefs, for instance, is necessary to apartheid theory and administration. In the past, chiefs governed always with a council of elders, a method that was traditionally patriarchal and excluded women and younger men. For the rest, though, it was not wholly undemocratic. Today the chiefs do not have legitimate authority exercised in taking decisions after long discussion with the elders; they are simply appointed civil servants, deposed if they do not carry out government orders and policies, and the council of elders no longer exists. In its place, the chief has headmen, whose role is to maintain 'law and order', as laid down by official policy.

Many other features of traditional African cultures, such as the absence of a money economy, or limitless cattle grazing, are in conflict with the requirements not only of an industrialised society, but also of apartheid. So the apartheid-created 'homelands' have a specious version of African custom and tradition imposed on them, and to these the people must conform.

This version, states sociologist H J Simons, reflects the authoritarian and patriarchal attitudes of the whites who devised it.[29] In particular, it incorporates many restrictions on women which are totally out of keeping with their modern attitudes, education, situation and needs — restrictions which, if they did exist in an earlier era, existed in conjunction with certain rights or safeguards that white legislators, administrators and judges now ignore.

Today, even in the bantustans, many women live outside the bounds of traditional society. Migrant labour and influx control regulations force them to become the heads of households; in a 1974 survey, 67 per cent of rural households were headed by women;[30] 80 per cent of households surveyed in the bantustan area of Bothashoek were headed by women.[31] Yet customary law as it has been institutionalised by whites places them perpetually under male tutelage, creating tremendous hardships. The contradictions that arise from this grafting of an old skin over a new framework place an intolerable burden on the whole African people, but most severely on African women.

Perpetual Minors

Until recently most African women had almost no legal capacities. Such changes as have so far taken place (described in more detail in a later section) have affected only a few. It was still the case in 1983 that the great majority ('99 per cent of married African women' according to one report[32]) were legal minors.

Women who are minors cannot own property in their own right, enter into contracts without the aid of their male guardian, or act as guardians of their own children. They are virtually perpetual minors, regardless of their age or marital status, always subject to the authority of men.

This is how customary law has been interpreted and applied by white courts. But it does not truly reflect the position of women in traditional society. According to H J Simons:

> Women had more rights as regards both their person and property than have been conceded to them by alien courts . . . Common law terms such as ownership, contract and status itself are saturated with an individualism alien to traditional African culture. Unless elaborately qualified, they distort the social relations underlying African legal rules. It would be closer to the mark to say that there was no law of contract, or

that ownership was unknown in tribal society, than to draw a distinction in these matters between the capacity of women and men.[33]

Initiative and the right to act rested with the family rather than the individual. There were clearly defined positions for each member, with claims and obligations, but the household constituted an integral whole. Neither man nor woman could normally exist outside a domestic group, and the activities of the sexes were complementary and not in conflict.

A woman shared her father's or husband's rank. She undertook much of the laborious work in the home and fields, not for an employer but for a family to which she and her children belonged. What she produced or acquired did not become the 'property' of her husband. It formed part of a joint family estate which he managed, not in the capacity of 'owner', but as head and senior partner.[34]

Women, though they occupied a subordinate position, occasionally attained a high degree of independence in some roles, such as those of diviner and herbalist, and occasionally in some tribes as chieftainess.

Each sex had its own sphere of activity, and women did not contend with men for power, rank or office because their roles were not competitive.

The concept of the independent woman or man cannot take shape in this kind of society. People see themselves as members of kinship groups, not as individuals with separate rights:

Something more than legal reforms is required to emancipate women from the patriarchal authority. The family must cease to be the main productive unit, and lose its self-sufficiency, women must receive modern education and participate, along with the men, in productive activity outside the home, before they can assert claims to equality of status.[35]

The colonial process weakened an authority that was in many ways conservative, breaking an integrated system and so freeing the individual from its constraints — and from its supports. The web of human relations was both stifling and sustaining. That women could survive this rupture and establish a new set of relations is evident in the degree of responsibility and independence that women have developed in the bantustans where men are absent; as they have done in the urban areas. But, according to a recent history, the colonial intrusion robbed women in more material ways. Women were further excluded by the colonial codification of tribal law; 'the colonists rigidified and exaggerated the subservience of African women under tribalism'.[36]

The concept of women as economic attachments to men is evident in the provisions made for women in the very important sphere of land, writes Cynthia Kros.[37] African women were deprived of their access to the means of production. Available land was given to men rather than to women.

So the existing methods of farming were radically changed, the division of labour distorted, while the old forms were retained and the content crumbled. With the bantustans already overcrowded and short of arable land, drained of much of their labour power by migrant labour, production declined rapidly and poverty became endemic.

Loneliness

The more fortunate woman in the rural areas of the bantustans has a husband working in the city. She attempts to feed the children, and probably other dependants, on the crops she cultivates from the small, barren family plot, if any, and the meagre amounts, if any, that are remitted by her husband. And this housewife, virtually a widow from the time she marries, lives out her lonely life, unable to leave, in a community composed largely of women, children, the aged and infirm who have been evicted from the cities under the pass laws once they become 'unproductive' labour units.

An African woman writes of the women of the bantustans:

> It is the tragic story of thousands of young women who are widows long before they reach the age of thirty; young married women who have never been mothers; young women whose life has been one long song of sorrow — burying one baby after another and lastly burying the husband — that lover she has never known as husband and father. To them — both men and women — adulthood means the end of life; it means loneliness, sorrow, tears and death; it means a life without future because there is no present.[38]

In the barren and particularly unproductive relocation areas, women may spend most of the day collecting firewood and carrying water from the nearest river or borehole, just to sustain day-to-day existence.

Land Hunger

The Economic Commission for Africa estimates that women provide 60 per cent to 80 per cent of all agricultural labour in Africa.[39] In South Africa, as in many other African countries, women make up the bulk of the agricultural workforce where agriculture is the mainstay of the economy. Women also suffer from the land hunger endemic in the bantustans. The shortage of land to support the population has been aggravated by the resettlement in the bantustans of Africans who have

30

been forcibly evicted from the cities, from the 'black spots' and white farm areas.

It should always be remembered that the official term 'resettlement' does not necessarily mean that the Africans brought to the bantustans came from there in the first place, or have ever been there. Most of the people in resettlement camps were born and lived all their lives in urban areas or other parts of the countryside. Dumping them into the bantustan increases the problem of insufficient land. But the local authorities are able to ignore a large proportion of such problems by their refusal to allocate land to women.

By law, allotments of land may be made to any married person or kraal-head (village head) who is officially a citizen of the particular bantustan or 'homeland'. A widow or unmarried woman with family obligations can be defined as a 'kraalhead', but the allocation of land is an administrative act that cannot be challenged in a court of law. Only a widow with children has any chance of being allocated land, and usually she will receive only half of the allocation made to a man.

A widow in occupation of her late husband's land forfeits her right to use the land if she remarries, or leaves her late husband's homestead, or refuses to live at another place agreed by his family.

A widow is expected to find money to pay for quitrent and local tax, and to buy food and clothing for herself and her children, out of the produce from the land, which may be no bigger than one or two acres. If she assumes the role of breadwinner and leaves her children in the bantustan to go to work for a wage, she runs the risk of losing her right to cultivate her holding.

Women in peasant communities cannot exist easily without land or without a father, husband or son to support them. The preference given to male kinsmen often imposes severe hardships on women who are passed over in favour of a brother or nephew of a deceased holder.

An obvious solution would be to allow unmarried daughters to use the plot in the absence of a male descendant, but the administration objects that this reform would make girls independent of male control and place a premium on 'spinster motherhood'. It is official policy to buttress the patriarchal authority. But the main source of the objection is the chronic and acute scarcity of land.[40]

Land scarcity, states Simons, is the major determinant of policy in the allocation of land. Women do most of the work in the fields; yet the administration insists that they are less productive.

But the main argument (in giving land preferentially to men) is the shortage of land and the need to provide land for men with families. The people reply that the country is full of widows, and ask how they are to support their children without land. The widows pay taxes like the men, and should have the same rights as men to change their place of residence. The people complain that the administration oppresses widows . . . There is often bitter competition between individual men and women for land, but the conflict stems from land hunger and not from tribal custom. The people want to restore to women the rights they had to land in the old society. But all attempts to bring about the change have failed to persuade an inflexible bureaucracy which is not responsible to the people.[41]

Lack of Jobs

Not only are there few jobs for women living in the bantustans, but there are barriers to obtaining work. Restrictions are imposed on their mobility, both by law and by the household responsibilities that, unlike the men, they cannot discard. Widows are afraid to leave their homes to seek work, as they will lose what rights they may have to cultivate family land. There are few secondary industries in the bantustans. Many of the women, having been denied access to education, are not only illiterate but frequently unable to speak either English or Afrikaans, an obstacle to all but the most unskilled physical labour.

In recent years 'border industry' jobs have been created on the fringes of some of the bantustans. These jobs, usually in small-scale craft or textile production, are done by women at the lowest end of the wage-scale *(see Part II)*.

Rural poverty, so conveniently hidden from visitors to towns and game parks, is constantly increased through the lack of investment and by the removal of male labour.

The increased restrictions since 1952 on the movement of women, administered by means of a system of labour bureaux and the influx control regulations, make it extremely difficult for them to leave the country areas. *(See Appendix for information about the labour bureau system.)* But despite the prohibitions on movement, starvation and their desperate conditions drive women to seek work, often illegally.

The bantustans are both reserves and reservoirs. They are reservoirs from which the apartheid regime can draw its supplies of labour at will, and they are reserves that must accept the unemployed, the old and disabled, all those women who have no function within the operation of apartheid; all those, in fact, who are not needed by the white-run economy.

Fruits of 'Independence'

With the decision of the apartheid regime to create official 'homelands', new conditions are being created that are even more to the disadvantage of the women. There are now four territories inside South Africa that the government has declared 'independent states'. They are: the Transkei, Venda, Bophuthatswana and Ciskei. Ciskei is the newest 'state', but it has lost no time in following the examples of the other three in bringing into being a brutal and oppressive administration, loyal to the apartheid regime, encompassing the same repressive legislation and violations of human rights as those imposed on the rest of South Africa.

No official declaration can transform these four client areas into 'independent nations'. Unrecognised by any country in the world, they are, and will remain, underdeveloped reserves set aside for African occupation within the total framework of apartheid strategy. However, the puppet bodies set up to administer the territories develop in their own way, and bring their own changes to the lives of people living there.

Within these bantustans are mirrored the undemocratic and male-dominated political structures of the white rulers, coupled with a superficial modernisation process based solely on the concepts of a profit economy. Practices considered to be 'traditional' are revived out of their historical and social context. Under the name of preserving the culture and traditions of the past, social progress is arrested and the traditional becomes the expression of the most conservative and repressive elements, who in turn are associated with the groups pressing for profitable and superficial 'modernisation'.

The first act of the Gazankulu bantustan — not yet declared 'independent' — was the legalisation of polygamy. The Transkei has introduced polygamy, and corporal punishment is extended to girls as well as boys.

As a bantustan politician in the Transkei emphasised in a speech in 1976, according to traditional law and custom women are perpetual minors, may not own property, nor decide affairs relating to their home kraal.[42]

Bophuthatswana is a 'nation' only in the minds of apartheid planners. It consists of seven separate blocks of land, scattered in three different provinces. Its dusty 'capital', Mmabatho, consists of a sprawling black ghetto, a luxury hotel with a casino, other luxury hotels for senior officials, and a parliamentary building and sports stadium. When it acquired its new status as a 'nation' in 1977, Mmabatho was the only 'capital city' in the world without even a row of shops.[43]

However, Bophuthatswana has found a bizarre way of making money. It has become the provider of forbidden fruit for white South Africans.

A hundred miles across the veld from Johannesburg, over a non-existent 'border', and you are in Sun City, South Africa's £50 million resort complex: a 588-room hotel; a Las Vegas-style structure of considerable vulgarity where the fruit machines and roulette wheels are backed by lavish sports and entertainment facilities, a game park; and in particular a 'Superbowl' auditorium[44] where international golfing stars, actors and entertainers perform. Here the whites escape the puritanical restrictions of the government they themselves keep in power, and enjoy all that is forbidden in their own 'white' South Africa: nudity, sex between black and white, pornographic films, uncensored magazines, and above all, gambling. In a country that does not permit cinemas to open on Sundays, where laws prohibit sex between people from different 'population groups', inside or outside marriage, where you can be fined £100 for possessing a ten-year-old copy of Playboy magazine, there is this enclave where legally anything goes.

Visitors to Sun City seldom drive off the main highway. They never see how the citizens of Bophuthatswana live. Winterveld, the shanty-town city, the lives of whose women residents are described in an earlier section on removals, lies within Bophuthatswana. Throughout the entire western area surrounding the 'capital' of Mmabatho lies a chain of re-location camps, some with only 400 people, others vast sprawls of 15,000 people. 'It seems a long cry from the million-dollar golfers in Sun City. But it's the same country, the same system, the same homeland.'[45]

II. Health, Welfare and the Family

II.1 Marriage and the Family

Marriage Laws

Colonialism brought a marked deterioration in the position of women, but especially in the position and status of married women. Their status and rights in the 'reserves' came to be determined by complicated rules arising out of customary law as interpreted by white judges and administrators and as affected by common and statute law. Laws affecting domestic relations vary to some extent in different areas; the most regressive, reactionary and repressive features of customary law as codified and construed by the white regime were incorporated into the Natal Code (Law No. 46 of 1887).

Africans in both town and country may choose to marry according to general South African law — 'common law' — or according to traditional law — 'customary union'. Marriage by common law is more usual in the towns; most Africans in the bantustans marry according to customary union.

Customary Union

African women must have parental consent to enter into a customary union. Such marriages are validated by *lobolo,* the transfer of cattle and/or money by the husband to the wife's father. In its earliest forms *lobolo* was not a bride-price so much as a 'child-price', whereby the cattle exchanges gave the husband claims to the wife's children as his own.

While some aspects of *lobolo* served a useful function in providing protection for married women, it had an essentially retrogressive aspect, curtailing the independence and freedom of women.

The wife who wished to leave her husband found it difficult to do so because rights to children were involved. Men who had come into ownership of cattle or children were not inclined to part with them merely because a woman wanted her freedom, and the only alternative left to the woman in the absence of a cattle refund from her father, was to give up her children. Even today, an African man may repudiate his marriage unilaterally simply by forfeiting his *lobolo* rights, but an African woman has no equivalent right.

Lobolo was thus one of the means whereby women were under the dominion of men in traditional society.

An African woman married by customary union is in most cases considered a minor under the tutelage of her husband. She cannot own property in her own right, except for her clothing and a few personal possessions; and if she earns money or in any way acquires property this becomes the property of her husband. She is unable to make a valid contract without her guardian's consent; or to sue or be sued. Her husband must do this on her behalf.

These laws vary somewhat according to the province. Under the Natal Native Code, for example, custody of the children can never be given to their divorced, separated or widowed mothers, even if it is the husband's conduct that caused the marriage break-up. Elsewhere, a divorced woman is deemed to have reached her majority, but under the Natal code a divorced woman is a perpetual minor, once more subject to the control of father or guardian, and she must live in his kraal. Her ex-husband keeps the children, though they must be allowed to stay with their mother until the age of about six.

Recent changes to the Natal Code, made in 1982 and 1983, have improved the situation of women in areas of Natal under the KwaZulu bantustan administration: these women now become legal majors on turning 21 and become able to enter into contracts without the permission of a male relative. The old Natal Code however continues to apply in the rest of Natal.[1]

Any woman may be confined to her kraal by a banning order issued by a Commissioner if he finds that she 'leads an immoral life', or being absent from her kraal is unable to 'give a good account of herself'.

The Minister of Bantu Administration and Development told Parliament in 1962 that one of the aims of his policy 'was to restore women to their rightful place as wife, mother, leader . . . the position that women occupied in the old society'.[2]

'In the name of restoring African women to their rightful place in that society, this specious culture over-emphasizes restrictions on women and distorts their role in rural society', says Elizabeth Landis. She concludes:

> Since various rights denied to African women under the Natal Code or married according to tribal law are granted without disastrous consequences to single women, it is apparent that these rights are not withheld for the protection of African women. However, to concede this would be to challenge the validity of the separate culture imposed on Africans — and, more importantly, to challenge the concept of separate culture

as a basic tenet of the South African political system. The Government consequently cannot countenance any fundamental amelioration in the status of rural African women, for such a reform would inevitably undermine apartheid.[3]

Common Law

Under common law, married women's rights over children and property depend on the choice made by the marriage partners. The marriage can be legalised by what is called 'community of property', or by the exclusion of community of property through a legally drawn antenuptual contract; or by marriage by customary union (see above).

All of these ways incorporate disadvantages for women, and involve their legal dependence.

To be married under community of property means that the husband acquires guardianship of the wife, who is considered a minor. He holds 'marital power', which means that a wife cannot enter into a binding contract or open a credit account without the prior permission of her husband. Until 1953 the husband could even take his wife's earnings, but the Matrimonial Affairs Act of that year alleviated the legal disabilities of married women. The wife's earnings are protected, although her husband may still take possession of anything she has bought with those earnings unless she obtains a court interdict against him.

An antenuptual contract excludes the husband's marital power and leaves his wife in full legal capacity in most matters.[4]

Although it is of advantage to them, the majority of women do not enter marriage with an antenuptual contract, either through ignorance, or because of the expense involved in having such a contract drawn up by a lawyer.

Many Africans go through two or even three forms of marriage: customary union, a civil marriage and, for some, a church marriage as well. When married by civil rites, African marriages are assumed to be out of community of property, unless a special declaration to the contrary is signed.

A new Matrimonial Property Act, which came into force in 1984[5] was lauded as a breakthrough for women. The new act abolishes marital power in marriages under common law, the power that makes husbands the sole administrator of family property and gives joint administration to husband and wife.

The drawback to this apparently progressive measure is that apart from the fact that it excludes all present community of property marriages from its reforms (unless the husband consents to the abolition of his marital power), it also excludes the majority of women — apart from a very few exceptions it does not apply to African married women (whose legal status was made a subject of investigation by the South African Law Commission appointed in 1983).[6]

The Family

In town and country today, South Africa teaches potent lessons in the meaning of the family, of patriarchy, of the exploitation of women. The illusion persists that the individual family is the basic economic unit of society. The conventional morality relating to the family, piously upheld by the state, by its propaganda, by its religious institutions, by its laws and its codes of ethics, is unrelated to reality. The establishment of bantustans, restrictions on women entering the towns, mass population removals, harsh laws relating to movement and work, and most of all, the spread of migrant labour, all these have had a devastating effect upon human relationships as expressed in terms of marriage and the family.

In 1968 the separation of migrant workers from their families was made more absolute by the introduction of a new system of contract labour. Prior to 1968 a migrant worker whose family had some access to land could work in the cities for a while and then spend some months with his family and working on his land before entering the labour market once more. The new 1968 system made it obligatory for migrants who wished to re-register in their jobs to return within 28 days. By law, a migrant must return to his home area to renew his contract, but may have little more than two weeks each year to live with his family. The new system has also weakened family relations among the workers themselves. In the past employers could specify the area from which they wished to recruit workers; now they may not, and can rarely name individuals whom they wish to recruit. Thus a migrant worker may no longer have his brothers, his sons, or other close relatives, coming to work in the same factory and live in the same hostel as himself.

'It is impossible,' wrote Sheena Duncan in 1983,

> for a migrant to bring his family legally to town to live with him, and the illegal residence option is becoming increasingly difficult to maintain as the administration of influx control becomes more efficient and the penalties more severe. The demolition of self-built shelters and homes now appears to be carried out systematically . . . and the ruthlessness with which the KTC* people were handled in Cape Town in May 1983 is a foretaste of the kind of action which can be anticipated in the future.

---

*'KTC' is the name of a site of a squatter camp.

An amendment to the Trespass Act made in 1983, which raised the penalties for this offence from R50 or three months in prison to R2,000 or two years' imprisonment, was another indication of what was in store.

The increasing number of landless people in the bantustans caused by the removal of people from the 'white' areas and their dumping in 'closer settlements' *(see Appendix)* has also led to a marked deterioration in family structures. If a family has some access to land and therefore to subsistence the permanent family unit has consisted of the children, women of all ages and old people, the able-bodied men being away working elsewhere. This unit may not have the qualities of a normal family group but it nevertheless provides some kind of stable nuclear unit with recognised structures.

> In the closer settlements where there is no land many family units consist only of a grandmother and a large number of children abandoned in her care. The younger women leave and disappear into the 'illegal' underground in the cities, returning infrequently to leave another illegitimate baby with the grandmother.[7]

In the urban areas outside the bantustans, Sheena Duncan explains, the destruction of the family has different roots but equally disastrous consequences. Apart from the familiar effects of rapid industrialisation, there are the laws that deny the right of families to live together, and the fact that the regime uses control over the provision of family accommodation as one of the main weapons in the armoury of influx control.

Local authorities were warned by the Deputy Minister of Bantu Administration in 1967 not to provide urban Africans with 'bigger, better, more attractive and more luxurious facilities, because it should be remembered that an urban Bantu residential area is not a homeland but part of a white area'.

Between 1968 and 1978 an embargo on the building of family housing was enforced. There has always been an acute shortage of housing for Africans in urban areas. Families with all the correct documentation and permits must wait many years for the allocation of a house, and meanwhile they will live as lodgers provided they have a permit for this, in the homes of others who must also have a permit to take in lodgers.

One consequence of the housing shortage is overcrowded houses. There were over 21,000 African families waiting for houses in Soweto alone in 1983 and a conservatively estimated national shortage in 1982 of 168,000 family units in urban areas outside the bantustans, according to a government commission in 1982, the Viljoen Commission. These figures do not reflect the real housing requirements as they do not include the thousands of families who are not legally entitled to rent or buy a house and who are unhoused.[8]

Estimates of the number of persons in the tiny Soweto houses vary, from 5.93 in 1977 by the Bureau of Market Research, to 14 quoted by the Johannesburg Chamber of Commerce in 1976; while the Black Sash office has suggested that the number is as high as 29.[9]

Three or four generations are often crammed into houses designed for a nuclear family unit. The gross overcrowding has changed and distorted the whole pattern of family life in the black community. There are even times, according to Sheena Duncan, when 'the fight to secure shelter leads to complete breakdown in trust and fondness between family members as each goes behind the other's back and the richest takes the house because he can afford to pay the biggest bribe'.[10]

Another consequence of the deliberately created housing shortage is the growth of squatter townships and the building of 'shacks' or unauthorised accommodation in official townships. Those families who are currently the victims of the nationwide demolition of self-built homes are the ones who have struggled hardest to maintain the bonds of family and stability. They are now being threatened and often defeated, by the ruthless determination of the authorities. Once the shelter is demolished the family is almost always divided because there is nowhere else they can find space to stay together.[11]

A family is not automatically re-united when it is allocated a house. If children were away at school at the time the parents applied for a house, their names would not be included on the house permit; others might have been living with relatives in rural areas. Once the parents finally obtain their home, permission to have the children with them is often refused.[12]

Women in Towns

Even with legal rights to reside in towns, black women live under the strains of great insecurity. Their legal status may be rescinded on a large variety of pretexts. A woman must avoid the misfortune of being left without a husband, whether through desertion, divorce or death. She often loses her home as well as her husband. A divorced woman may be given permission to stay in her home only if she was not the guilty party in the divorce suit, and has been granted custody of the children; if she qualifies in her own right to remain in town; if she can pay the rent; and if her former husband has agreed to vacate the house. If he has remarried immediately, he may choose to remain in the house with his new wife.

African women who are living lawfully in an urban area outside a bantustan may only obtain work through the municipal or district labour officer, from whom they must obtain a permit. Labour officers can refuse to issue a permit for many reasons, or they may refuse a permit for a specific job that a woman wishes to take and refer her to another somewhere else; or they may require women, with their dependants, to leave the area. A labour officer can also cancel an existing labour contract, a provision that hangs over the head of those African workers (male or female) who may participate in trade union or political activities.

Particularly if she is unemployed, a woman must avoid any activity which would make her fall within the definition of an 'idle Bantu' in Section 29 of the Urban Areas Act. In terms of that law (under challenge in the courts in 1983 and 1984) the definition includes any African woman other than a 'bona fide housewife', between the ages of 15 and 60, and who, even if supported by her parents, is normally unemployed although capable of working (unless she is a student). It also includes women who refuse jobs offered by the labour office, or who are fired from their jobs too frequently. Refusal to accept employment offered by a labour bureau without 'acceptable' reasons, or being dismissed too frequently are also grounds for being declared 'idle'. A person held to be an 'idle Bantu' is ordered to be removed from the urban area, and sent to the bantustans.

A woman must also avoid conduct which will lead an urban authority to hold her presence as 'detrimental to the maintenance of peace and order' and therefore make her liable to removal.

Every African woman is painfully aware of the official attitude repeatedly expressed, that married women, children and older people are 'superfluous appendages', to be removed from the urban area as quickly as possible, even if they are technically qualified under Section 10 *(see Appendix)*. Single African girls living with their parents lose the right to stay in an area unless they were born there or the man they are marrying has the right to stay permanently in the area. And they may only live with the man they are marrying provided he has the appropriate residence rights.

A work permit may also be refused to a woman if she is unable to find housing, and the women are under severe difficulties as houses are not usually available for women. Hostels and compound accommodation are for men, with the exception of a few township hostels.

Many unhappily married women suffer, unable to take any action, knowing that if their husbands desert or divorce them, they may lose their right to live with their children as well.

An African woman is even subject to arrest for living with her husband if he stays with her in domestic servant's quarters, or if she cohabits with him in his quarters when he is not qualified to have his family with him.

Hostel Life

Not a great deal of detailed information is available on the subject, but some African women, as well as the men who form the bulk of the hostel-dwellers, are made to live in single-sex hostels. This is the accommodation which the apartheid system imposes on those forced to be migrant workers and on many single people who live in urban areas outside the bantustans.

Women living in hostels are mainly domestic workers or workers in industry, as well as widows, divorcees, orphans or unmarried mothers.

The practice of accommodating migrant workers in single-sex barrack-like quarters goes back to the beginning of large-scale mining in South Africa. From the 1950s there was a great expansion of this practice with the construction of hostels in many townships, including hostels for women.

It was decided in 1962 to establish, nine miles outside Johannesburg, in Alexandra township, the most dramatic prototype of the new life that was being planned. The scheme to replace all family accommodation with single-sex accommodation for workers involved moving all families out of the area and moving in men and women living alone in the white suburbs of Johannesburg and in servants' quarters in blocks of flats for whites ('locations in the sky'). By 1964 more than half the population of Alexandra had been removed. Eight hostels, each to house 2,500 people were planned. Among the first to be built in 1972 was one to accommodate 2,800 women.[14]

By that time a hostel for women had also been built in Orlando West in Soweto, a smaller one which in 1980 had 800 residents.[15]

Life in hostels is harsh, restrictive and oppressive. There are few facilities for leisure; shared rooms for most residents; and in most cases no provisions for children of mothers or husbands of married women to visit. Equally, male hostels have no rooms for wives to stay or children to visit. The exceptions are a few, mainly new, hostels in which improvements in some conditions have been made, while the basic principles of single-sex hostel accommodation have been preserved.[16]

Women have resisted living in hostels, and in fact the women's hostel in Alexandra had not been filled by 1980. (The scheme to convert the whole of Alexandra to a complex of hostels was itself abandoned in 1979, only partly completed.[17]) Resistance came from women not only because of the poor conditions in the hostels, but more fundamentally because of the disruption of personal relations and the fragmentation of family life involved.

Since the children could not stay in the hostels, mothers were unwilling to become hostel dwellers. Some women were so desperate for a roof over their heads together with their children that they would stay illegally in the townships, paying admission of guilt fines whenever raided by the police. Others stayed in houses due to be demolished, moving on again and again when the bulldozers came.[18]

I lived in a women's hostel where most of the women had children. Many could barely sleep worrying about where their children were staying — with strangers, or old grannies — paying out most of their money so their children could survive. Still they could not see them. This experience turned me around . . . If the government had set out to create a society that would consume itself, it couldn't have done better. It has destroyed our family life, left the homelands fatherless with mothers struggling to help the remains of their family survive. Either the women must go mad or revolt.

(A woman describing her reaction to hostel life — 'The Role of Women in the Struggle for Liberation in Zimbabwe, Namibia & South Africa', Paper presented at UN Conference on Women, Copenhagen, 14-30 July 1980)

Many, though, were unable to continue their resistance indefinitely. If they did not qualify under the pass laws for a house, they were faced with the alternative of having to go to a bantustan or to enter the hostels. Three-quarters of so-called 'single' women in the Alexandra hostel had children. Four out of five of the children went to bantustans, and the rest went to live with relatives in the towns or on white-owned farms.[19]

Occasional reports in the press indicate that the women who live in the hostels continue to resist and protest. In particular, over 350 women in the Alexandra hostel signed a petition in 1980 protesting at the fact that they were not allowed visitors. They also protested that some of them had school-going children living with relatives in the townships who were not allowed to visit their mothers in the hostel rooms.[20]

The residents have complained, too, of other conditions — for example, inadequate heating and lighting, high rents, and their vulnerability to violence from criminal men.[21] The authorities have responded to some of these complaints. It has also been reported that both private and public sector employers plan to improve conditions in hostels and make provision for visits from husbands or wives 'to stay for a few days'. But there are no signs that hostels, or the migrant labour system of which they are a part, are to be abandoned.[22]

Independence

The enormous gap between the idealised theory of the family and the brutal reality under apartheid has resulted in the emergence of the independent woman. In both town and countryside African women often find themselves heads of households and particularly in urban conditions this has had spreading effects on social relations. Still totally dependent in terms of law and of patriarchal customs, they find themselves in actuality forced into a bitter independence, forced to become the responsible ones, the decision-makers. And the results of this situation have changed their status and will make an important impact on relationships in the future.

A Johannesburg journalist, Percy Qoboza, maintains that the picture painted of the black woman as a depressed, voiceless, subservient person is misleading and often dangerous. He describes the historical background of their militant struggles against political oppression, and says black women are not the subservient objects many people take them to be.

> We continue to insult their dignity and motherhood in various ways. Getting them to clean pavements in Soweto is an affront to their dignity . . . throwing them in jail in Hillbrow for not having passes degrades their dignity. Their silent endurance of these insults must not be taken for subservience.[23]

The truth is that to survive, black women have had to develop a high degree of independence and to exert great strength of character. Sociologists have commented on the emergence of the single, independent, black woman. Speaking on the 'changing status of African women' Professor Monica Wilson of the University of Cape Town said that women's rights were destroyed more by the fact that they were part of a disenfranchised community than that they were women. 'The most pressing disability of African women is the restriction on the rights of movement and residence which prohibits their joining their husbands who are working in the towns. . . . Why be tied to a man who will be continually absent?'[24]

A black newspaper editor, Mr Tom Moerane, reports on research undertaken by his daughter among African women.

> A significant number of young women regarded marriage in an entirely negative manner. They said they did not care about marriage as an institution, nor did they think it was of any particular use to them. Some indicated that they desired to bear children and that this made it necessary to cohabit with a man, but 'the baby is going to be my baby'.[25]

In both town and country numbers of African women see dubious advantages in marriage and more and more young women show a preference for staying single. 'Girls who are married and have husbands in cities', comments a rural woman, 'are struggling as I do. Many are suffering as I do and yet have husbands.'[26] Joanne Yawitch says this tendency can be interpreted in many ways, but it does seem clear that the economic rewards of marriage are steadily declining. Furthermore, the fact that there is a gross contradiction in terms of who is *supposed* to take responsibility and decisions, and who *actually* does, often makes marriage an unviable option for rural women. Their reaction to the idea of marriage is 'highly ambiguous, contradictory and often aggressive'.[27]

The overcrowding, crime, poverty and increasing unemployment that are the features of township life impose massive strains on individuals. 'The family functions as a soak pit to absorb expressions of anger that are not allowed elsewhere. Often, men have had a hard day at work, get drunk and take it out on their wives and children. Battery and alcoholism are the most common results of this situation.'[28] In Soweto 60 per cent of children are illegitimate, and while parents may often marry after they are born, more women are choosing not to marry.

Whatever the complexity of reasons (including, in the urban areas, the tendency for women to be able to enter better-paid work than domestic service, decreasing their economic dependence on men) more and more women are finding marriage a burden to them.

The official census figures, already referred to above, are consistent with such a change. Whereas the proportion of white women who were married increased very slightly in the decade between 1970 and 1980 (from 45.1 per cent to 45.7 per cent) the much lower proportion of African women who were married (only 28.2 per cent in 1970) fell still further to 23.3 per cent in 1980.[29]

II.2 Children

Children are Illegal

Children, no matter how young, may not live with their mothers if those mothers are resident in one of the hostels, or 'living in' as domestics to a white family, even though domestic servants must live in a room that is actually separated from the main house. To prevent sympathetic employers from breaking this regulation by permitting a small child to live with its mother in domestic service, heavy fines are now imposed on the employers, as well as the penalties that are inflicted on the mother who illegally wishes to keep her baby or small child with her.

Women in Randburg, near Johannesburg, who come from the neighbouring bantustan of Bophuthatswana to work on contract, must sign an undertaking 'not to introduce' their children into the area.[30]

Once they reach the age of 16, children may not continue to live with their parents unless they qualify for urban residence in their own right — not because of the rights of a parent or parents. They must go to the bantustans — as the authorities say, 'sent back' — even if they have never been there in their lives, even if they have no relatives nor contact with anyone there. Many children in the towns are not so registered, for a number of reasons. Sometimes the authorities simply refuse to put a child's name on the permit; sometimes mothers are unable to produce a certificate showing the child was born in the area. Many babies are delivered by relatives and neighbours, and registration of African births is not compulsory. Where mothers are illiterate they may be ignorant of the provisions that will ultimately govern their children's lives. An illiterate mother who is given a form to fill in — evidence in years to come — by the local clinic may ignore it. Sometimes the mother is unmarried, and therefore not entitled to have any children on her permit.

The name of every man, woman and child in a house must appear on the permits. When black townships in urban areas are cleared and the residents moved, all who lack the necessary permits, tax receipts or papers are arrested; in many cases the husband has a job and qualifies for urban residence under Section 10, while his wife and children do not. Police raids are carried out day and night to remove the 'unqualified', and often women are arrested when their husbands are at work, leaving even small children totally alone.

When the press published stories of such children during the clearing of Alexandra Township, outside Johannesburg in 1972, Mr Coen Kotze, manager of the local board, stated: 'They are given ample time to make up their minds. We are giving them the choice: they must send their children back to the homelands themselves . . . this is the policy and we will enforce it.' The children, he said, who were being ordered out were *illegal*; and if the mothers were working, they were migrant workers recruited from the homelands on a single basis. 'The law states that they are illegally in the area, so they have to go. It's as simple as that.'[31]

African mothers living with their 'illegal' children are in constant dread of being found out, and to make matters worse, only those children can be registered for school who are listed on a residential permit which is impossible to procure if the mother is living in the urban area illegally.[32]

From this abrogation of family life flow results that are deeply destructive, but difficult to assess in any statistical sense. In the early 1970s it was stated that in Britain one child in every 14 was illegitimate. Sheena Duncan states that some sixty per cent of urban African children are illegitimate. In addition, many children are forced by poverty in the rural areas to seek existence in the alleys and doorways of the country's cities.[33]

II.3 Social Security

Under apartheid social security for black people, in particular Africans, is provided at such a negligible level that it makes little, if any, impact on the conditions of life. Only a small number of people fall within the requirements that make them eligible for such benefits.

This situation is an aspect of the creation of the migrant labour system. By preserving the subsistence sector from which migrant male labour was extracted in growing numbers and in which women were to predominate, labour could be acquired at a very low cost. Costs normally contributed to by the employers were met, if at all, by that sector. 'In real terms, women provide what otherwise would be called unemployment insurance, pension funds, education and health and sickness benefits, etc.'[34]

However, in reality the subsistence sector has been destroyed by apartheid. The lack of land, the mushrooming of populations through resettlement and the general conditions of extreme poverty make it impossible for families in the bantustans to produce what they need in the absence of such services.

The majority of black women workers are excluded from unemployment insurance by the limitations on those who may qualify. Domestic and agricultural workers — the majority of women workers — are excluded. So are seasonal workers and those whose earnings are calculated on a commission basis. The benefits paid amount to 45 per cent of the weekly earnings, for a maximum of 26 weeks per year.[35]

All pension applications are processed in Pretoria and take between six months and a year to finalise. African widows do not qualify for maintenance grants in rural areas, although such grants are available to widows of other groups.[36]

The maximum monthly pension for Africans in 1984 was R65 in comparison to R166 for whites. An African person's monthly income must not exceed R27 a month if he or she is to qualify for old-age pensions, whereas for whites the income can be R84. Pensioners living in urban areas outside bantustans who wish to qualify must prove they are living there lawfully. They must also provide documentary proof of their age, which many old people are not able to do. Even when pensions have been approved they may be arbitrarily withdrawn if the district administrator decides proof is insufficient.[37]

Because of the principle that the aged must return to the bantustan areas, facilities for their care scarcely exist outside the bantustans.

The situation for women in the bantustans is particularly bad; those who are entitled to pensions, and rely on the small amounts as their only means to survive, have little means of obtaining them if they do not arrive. Many are illiterate. To get someone to write a letter for them, to be able to afford the postage, or the fare to the local office, is often beyond their means.

A very low proportion of Africans, compared with other groups, receive pensions in South Africa, yet their dependence for survival on pensions is the highest of all groups. In 1977 257,663 Africans received pensions at the rate of R20.50 per month; 173,448 whites, at the rate of R79 per month; 120,611 Coloureds and 26,963 Indians, at the rate of R42.50 a month. Most pensions were for old age or disability. Child maintenance grants were not given in the bantustans.[38]

In many ways women constitute, as one writer recently put it, 'society's shock-absorbers', in the sense that in the absence of adequate social services the harsher and more restrictive conditions imposed by mass unemployment and by inflation fall most heavily on the shoulders of those who are responsible for administering the family's needs — the women.[39] Their domestic work increases, they must spend more time repairing old clothes and 'making do', they have to find ways of preparing cheaper meals, and in the urban areas many more are economically active than in the past.

II.4 Control of Fertility — or Populations

Women need to be able to control their own fertility. But when birth control becomes population control as it has in South Africa, it acquires a new significance. The total control over population that apartheid seeks to obtain in all fields extends to this area of social relations.

Contraception

The Dutch Reformed Church (DRC), the largest church in South Africa, is the theological and ideological power base of the regime. In 1960, a DRC spokesman on moral questions stated:

> The Church is generally opposed to birth control among whites on Christian and ethical grounds, and I suppose the same would be applied to Africans. This aspect has never been discussed by the church. But we do not consider the argument that the population may become too large is valid. Science and technology will cope.[40]

However, some years later when the decision was taken to distribute the contraceptive pill freely, DRC theologians had already adjusted to a new position. 'It is the duty of whites to multiply on the earth . . . and thus keep the increase of the white population high.' They would like to ban the pill for all white women. The pill leads to promiscuity and prostitution. However, 'the bantu . . . could be given the pill with an easy mind . . . the morals of the blacks have already sunk so low that promiscuity could not be any greater'.[41]

Responding to a claim that the country's crippling drought could increase the infant mortality rate, the Health Minister, Dr Nak van der Merwe, blamed 'uncontrolled breeding' for the high death rate among malnourished children, in a statement in April 1983 that called for the reduction of the black birth rate to two children per woman by the year 2020.[42]

Dr J de Beer, Director-General of the South African Department of Health and Social Welfare, expressing concern about the continuing increase in the black population despite the high infant mortality rate in some areas, stated, 'It is not easy to get the birth rate down other than by penalising people and having sterilisation and abortion both on demand and by command.'[43]

By January 1982, the Reformed Church was reported to be planning 'an information campaign to counter a declining number of white births in South Africa'.[44]

The white attitude to birth control is thus conditioned by racialist beliefs, and this found expression in a symposium on the 'population explosion' in South Africa organised by the Northern Transvaal Branch of the South African Medical Association in 1971. Dr Chris Troskie, a past president of the Medical Association, set forth a thesis that there were two basic groups among mankind, the 'haves' and the 'have-nots', the former group being intelligent, with a sense of responsibility and civilisation; the latter lacking responsibility and 'breeding recklessly'. The genetic composition of the population, determined at birth, had to be improved by eliminating inferior genetic material, and he argued for the sterilisation of defective people. Dr N J van Rensburg, deputy Superintendent of the H F Verwoerd Hospital in Pretoria, likened population growth to cancer which, if curative measures are not taken, spreads through the whole body and destroys it.[45]

The Family Planning Association (FPA) was formed in 1932 to provide voluntary birth control services; it joined the International Planned Parenthood Federation in 1953 and for a number of years battled against resistance to contraception at all levels of society. Objections on religious, moral and medical grounds existed among white and black people. Social factors influenced African men, such as loss of social status in the community and loss of bride-price. Women feared the anger of their men if their use of contraceptives was discovered, and many women were unable to obtain information about contraception because clinics would insist on the man's consent.

In 1966 the FPA received its first government grant, and in the six years to 1972, it transferred its 229 clinics to local authorities as soon as they were established. The FPA provides lectures, films, slide shows, comics and pamphlets to spread its message. Whites are drawn in to help 'educate' blacks with whom they have contact. An advertisement in a woman's magazine, *Fair Lady,* shows a white woman in her kitchen with the black domestic servant in the background. 'Family planning is my baby too!' the white woman says, and goes on to explain that as an employer her duties don't stop at paying her domestic a good salary, or providing her with food, clothing and a roof over her head. They go beyond to a 'sincere interest in her family life'. So she discusses family planning with her maid, and takes her to the nearest clinic, and thus has a more efficient and devoted domestic.[46]

Health Department propaganda shows happy, prosperous families with only two or three children, side by side with poverty-stricken families with many children. These images are used on posters, in comics and advertisements, with the clear implication that success, good jobs, smart clothes and money are the inevitable consequence of limiting family size. The General Secretary of the white-controlled trade union congress, Arthur Grobbelaar, sees birth control as a solution to unemployment: 'The long-term solution is birth control.'[47]

The Health Department pays for the training of nurses as well as the drugs used by the FPA clinics — but it will not support the cytology laboratory of the FPA in Johannesburg.[48] The rate of cervical cancer in South Africa was stated in 1983 to be 35.6 per 1,000 women screened (the year for which these figures applied was not stated).[49]

Of the entire Health Department, the only division that printed its pamphlets in every South African language was 'Family Planning'. A study undertaken by Barbara Klugman in a rural area in 1980, the Bochum area of the Lebowa bantustan, revealed that three out of five children in the area had pellagra, arising from malnutrition, and that there had been a recent epidemic of typhoid — from lack of adequate sanitation. Yet there were no campaigns on these issues which include pertinent literature in every language.[50]

Only an estimated two per cent of expenditure on health care service was devoted to preventative medicine.[51]

In theory contraception is free and available to all women; but availability is dependent on access to clinics, and despite the fact that there are 3,000 such clinics, women in remote rural areas are less likely to have such access, or the means to travel to the nearest clinic.

South Africa was one of the testing grounds for injectible contraceptives, like the controversial Depo Provera which has been banned in several countries, such as neighbouring Zimbabwe, and since 1978 the USA because of evidence that it has harmful side effects and may cause cancer. The manufacturers, Upjon Pharmaceutical Co., continue to market the drug in 76 countries. Dr Nthato Motlana, a Soweto physician, has stated: 'The developed world is dumping Depo Provera on the Third World, and government-funded agencies are administering the drug to young black women without their consent.'[52] Its convenience over other forms of contraception in ill-educated and rural populations is high. It is

50

injected once every three or six months and is irreversible — nothing can be done until the drug ceases to be active. It is cheap and easy to administer. But without doubt the side effects have not been adequately studied, nor its possible effects on the foetus or the breast-fed baby. D-P is used throughout South Africa and the routine of the mobile clinic in rural areas is governed by the period at which Depo Provera injections are given — namely, a visit to each farm, once every three to six months.[53]

Experience both in South Africa and in other countries shows that women do want to know about birth control, and readily accept it when women's organisations or local midwives give the instructions. There is no simplistic solution to the problem of birth control; medical, religious, moral and cultural factors and standards of living all play a part in forming attitudes. But the issues could only be resolved in a society that would give women status, education and health facilities.

Abortion

Abortion is virtually illegal in South Africa, although the Abortion and Sterilisation Act of 1975 legalised abortion in certain very closely controlled situations. These are: if there is a threat to the permanent mental or physical health of the mother or child; if pregnancy is a result of rape (see below) or incest; or if the mother is an imbecile.[54] Approval must be obtained from at least three doctors, one of whom must be a state-employed psychiatrist where the mental health clinic is involved. As there are only 27 state-employed psychiatrists in the country, this makes access difficult for many.

Assessing the effect of this law for the twelve months following its introduction, the president of an abortion reform group told a conference that the Act had failed; during this period, only 570 medical abortions had been performed, most of them on white women: amongst the 570 patients there were 402 White, 56 Coloured, 8 Asian and 21 African. She put the number of backstreet abortions 'conservatively' at 100,000, a figure also given more recently by a professor of law.[55]

Information about illegal abortions is difficult to obtain, but there are some indications. Approximately 25 per cent of all bed space in gynaecological wards in South Africa is occupied by women suffering complications following back-street or self-induced abortions, and it has been estimated that as many as 70 per cent of the deaths in gynaecological wards in 1976 were due to incomplete abortions.[56] The Centre for Applied Social Sciences in Natal estimated that in 1970 alone approximately 141,800 black women and 17,800 white women resorted to abortion.[57] Baragwanath Hospital (near Soweto, Johannesburg) runs two special wards at weekends to treat incomplete abortions. The Groote

Schuur Hospital in the Cape was forced to support a special septic abortion unit which had the highest bed occupancy and highest patient turnover of any ward in the hospital.[58] The King Edward VII Hospital in Natal treated over 4,000 septic abortion cases in 1972.[59] According to one newspaper report in 1981 hundreds of South African women were going to an 'abortion factory' across the border in Lesotho, where the superintendent of the Government Hospital at Teyateyaneng, a doctor from South Korea, performed abortions for R400.[60]

II.5 Rape

It is extremely difficult to obtain accurate figures of the incidence of rape. By far the largest number of rapes take place against black women in the violent and degraded conditions in the urban townships where the police are more concerned with the suppression of resistance and the enforcement of apartheid than with crime prevention. Many cases go unreported and those cases that are reported may not be dealt with seriously by the police.

The figures given here come from different sources. A Medical Association of South Africa report states that a woman is raped every three minutes in South Africa — 300,000 annually.[61] Official (police) statistics of reported rape cases have been given as 14,600 per annum — 40 a day.[62] Another source reports 14,953 reported rape cases in 1977, of which 14,242 were of 'non-whites by non-whites', making up 95 per cent of the total.[63] In 1980, 15,000 rapes were recorded by the Department of Law and Order,[64] and the National Institute for Crime Prevention and the Rehabilitation of Offenders states that 400 women are raped every single day, a horrific figure, they say, of which only some 20 cases are actually reported. Jacklyn Cock has put the daily figure at almost double that: 777 women raped every day in South Africa.[65]

Mr Roland Graser, director of the National Institute for Crime Prevention and the Rehabilitation of Offenders, stated that the rape figure for 1976 should stand at 292,000 per annum, with an estimated 2,920 rape-associated abortions.[66] As the official statistics for that year showed only 539 legal abortions for all causes, of which 399 were performed on white women, it would appear that women are either refused the right to legal abortion, or too intimidated by the intricacies of the requirements to ask for legal terminations; or else remain in ignorance of the fact that they have a right to termination.[67]

In the United States it is estimated that only one in ten rape cases are reported; however, in South Africa the estimate of reported cases is only one in twenty; and rape has the lowest conviction rate of any crime of violence in the country.[68] In the Cape Flats — an area of shanties and slum housing — it was estimated that the figures could be as high as one in thirty.[69]

A 'Rape Crisis' report from Cape Town reported 41,341 men prosecuted for rape in a four-year period. Of these, 22,408 were convicted, and 19 were sentenced to death. The youngest rape victim was three, the eldest seventy. There were 41 cases of children under seventeen.[70]

The rape of a white woman by a black man is a serious crime that can result in sentence of death. Rape of black women is treated as a minor offence. In reported cases police themselves are frequently involved in the rape of black women, often of those who have been arrested on some pretext. As in other countries, humiliating police interrogation, unsympathetic medical examinations and harassment by lawyers discourage women from proceeding with charges of rape. To this must be added the context of blatant racial prejudice, often expressed openly in obscene language by the police towards black women.

Representatives of rape clinics meeting in Johannesburg in 1982 made suggestions of law changes in the case of rape, the definition of which was far too narrow. It was said that the crime of 'rape' should be supplanted by a broader category of 'sexual assaults', which would help to remove the stigma of rape, making victims feel freer to report incidents. One of the main reasons that many rape cases were not reported, stated a representative, was because the crime of rape carried the maximum penalty of the death sentence. 'In some cases the rapist is known to the victim and she is reluctant to report the case, realising the person could be hanged.'[71]

II.6 Health and Poverty in the Countryside

Infant mortality rates (IMR) — that is, the number of babies who die before their first birthday, per 1,000 live births — are usually accepted as a reliable guide to the general state of health and health services in a country. The problem in South Africa is that apartheid does not collect national figures for Africans; the figures shown in Table V are based on surveys in different parts of the country. By comparison the numbers of deaths per 1,000 live births in Britain in 1980 was 12 and the number for Canada in 1981 was 9.6.[73]

The white population of South Africa enjoys an extremely high standard of health care. There are no malnutritional diseases to be found among them, there is a more than adequate supply of doctors, and hospitals have a high reputation for their treatment of their white patients. The infant mortality rate for whites is among the lowest compared with the highly developed countries of the western world.

African women in rural areas have heavy and often lonely responsibilities. The lives of most of them are defined by poverty, unemployment and landlessness and this is reflected in the diseases suffered by them and by those they are responsible for.

The women are responsible for the care and feeding of the children when so many families are without fathers. Often there are no hospitals or clinics available in distant country areas.

Too often in conditions of extreme poverty, women starve themselves rather than their families. Tension-related illnesses and mental breakdowns are the outcome, and daily tasks of a very hard physical nature (fetching water from long distances, for example) are often carried out by very young or very old women.

Medical facilities, when available, are not free; the R3 needed for hospital attention or the R1 for clinics may mean that the women postpone attending as long as possible. Long distances have to be travelled to seek medical assistance. Maternity care is often totally absent, and delivery and ante-natal care are costly and beyond the reach of many.

Health workers explaining the need for balanced diets, regular examination and sanitation may only increase the guilt that the women feel for the illnesses of their families.[75]

The problem in assessing health conditions of the black population is the lack of statistics, and in particular the fact that the little information that is available is not broken down by sex. But there is enough information to indicate some of the problems for women in rural areas, where they rear children and care for the aged under difficult circumstances.

After I started to have children I began to feel the hardship. For example, if a child fell sick it would take time for me to write to my husband and for him to reply and all the time the child would be getting worse. By the time I received money from my husband to pay the doctor the doctor would be angry that I had not brought the child before . . . Perhaps I would be able to purchase only one bottle of medicine with the money I was sent and then not be able to take the child back to the doctor. This happend with my first child but when this happened to my second child my husband advised me to come to Cape Town.

(A woman who went 'illegally' to Cape Town in defiance of the pass laws — 'The Effects of Apartheid on the Status of Women', Paper presented at UN Conference on Women, Copenhagen 14-30 July 1980)

Malnutrition

Nutritional diseases such as kwashiorkor are no longer notifiable, and so it is not easy to estimate their scale. But among the African population malnutrition has reached epidemic proportions, a fact that has been recorded in numerous studies.[76]

54

In 1966, the last year in which kwashiorkor was a notifiable disease, official figures mentioned 11,000 cases.[77] In 1980, it was found that in one area alone in Pietermaritzburg, 40 children died every day from kwashiorkor or marasmus.[78]

The extent of malnutrition was underlined in a paper to a United Nations Conference in 1980:

> Malnutrition has assumed crisis proportions in South Africa and, with the price of essential daily food such as bread and milk rising, there is every possibility that hunger will rage through the deprived black community of South Africa like a dreadful scourge. Indeed the prospect for blacks is grim and forbidding . . . 75 children (African and Coloured) are dying every day from lack of proper and adequate food.[79]

More recently, in 1983, Professor Allie Moosa estimated that 30,000 children die of malnutrition every year, and that between two and three per cent of the eight million black children in South Africa are suffering from malnutrition. Forty-five per cent of all children admitted to the King Edward VII Hospital in Durban suffered from malnutrition, and about one in five dies, Professor Moosa stated.[80] Reacting to this report the Minister of Health, Dr Nak van der Merwe, said that responsibility for a high toll of dying children should be shared by those who breed uncontrollably. He said the problem of three of four children dying every hour was intimately tied to the socio-political situation.[81]

The South African Institute of Race Relations stated in 1983 that the government's population removal programme has helped to destroy subsistence agriculture and has contributed to the 'staggeringly high' black infant mortality rates which were a direct result of apartheid policies.[82]

Dr Jack Penn, one of the world's leading plastic surgeons, stated in 1981:

> . . . the battle against malnutrition is becoming climacteric. For example, children who are burned and require skin grafts, must have their surgical treatments delayed until their nutrition has been brought to a suitable standard. In cases where malnutrition has been a feature since birth this may be almost impossible and the risk of infection and slow healing is always a problem. Moreover, even though the child may make good progress while well cared for and fed, on returning to the home environment, the lack of adequate nutrition may cause a breakdown of his wound.[83]

The trauma and agony of coping with these children, of being unable to provide them with sufficient food, of watching their deteriorating conditions, of digging graves and putting up small wooden markers over the place of burial in stony land — all this falls on the shoulders of the women.

Patterns of Disease

One of the world's six most formidable diseases, cholera, usually gets a hold in populations living without a purified water supply. The source is most likely to be water contaminated by human excrement. In the past few years cholera, after being absent for many years from South Africa, has appeared in resettlement areas; the first outbreak occurred in the KaNgwane bantustan in the eastern Transvaal in 1980. Six weeks after the first case was confirmed, 28 people had died from cholera, and a few months later it was estimated that well over half the population of 80,000 had been infected. By the end of the year a second cholera epidemic was spreading in the 'homelands' — this time in Bophuthatswana and KwaZulu.

As well as cholera, typhoid epidemics occur with increasing frequency in resettlement areas. The dumping-grounds have become death camps in which not only cholera and typhoid, but other diseases — gastro-enteritis, poliomyelitis, tuberculosis, malaria, as well as diseases of starvation, such as kwashiorkor, marasmus and pellagra — flourish. These diseases are usually associated with severe poverty in countries that lack developed resources and basic amenities. Yet they are found in rich, prosperous South Africa.

In the same year, 1981, it was estimated that 50,000 children would die of malnutrition in the rural areas with another 100,000 children's lives at risk.[84] Malnutrition takes many different forms: kwashiorkor is a disease resulting from protein deficiency; marasmus and pellagra are prevalent, and less commonly, rickets, scurvy, beri-beri and anaemia.

In 1978 there were 42,785 new cases of tuberculosis reported in South Africa. Communicable diseases play havoc with malnourished young bodies, so that a high rate of tuberculosis, typhoid, tetanus, measles, polio, diptheria, hepatitis and pertussis are common. Measles in South Africa kills more children in three days than it does in the United States in one year. A press report in 1983 noted 100 deaths in three months of black children in Port Elizabeth, from measles. Soweto has the highest recorded incidence of rheumatic fever in the world.

During the first ten years of the existence of Limehill, a resettlement area in Natal, 11 per cent of the children who were aged five years or less at the time of removal were dead. It was described by the people living there as 'a land of sorrows'.

Mental Health

It is not only a question of physical health.

It is unthinkable that racism would be without implications for mental health. Healthy mental functioning and personality development depend on the presence and continuity of such essential experiences as the individual's sense of security and worth, freedom for personal growth and identification with a community of equals. Racism undercuts at the roots of healthy mental life by depriving its victims of these experiences and by conditioning them into accepting the myth that the cause of their inferior status in society lies irrevocably within themselves.[85]

Migrant labour is the cause of much of the mental illness experienced by Africans, women in particular. This is clearly stated in a study by a group of black doctors:

There can be no doubt that the migrant labour system is damaging to the mental well-being of black people. This enforced separation of migrant labourers in city hostels from their families in the homelands has destroyed the fabric of traditional African society and robbed Africans of the fundamental human right of working and living within the security and comfort of their own families.

Mothers and children in the ethnic 'homelands' are denied the fulfilment provided by the presence of the husband and father. The emotional and intellectual deprivation of this enforced and totally inhumane separation must result in incalculable harm to the family unit.[86]

Breakdowns in health are not confined to physical symptoms, according to research on resettlement problems in KwaZulu.[87] The resettlement experience is extremely traumatic, particularly because the people being resettled are generally uneducated and illiterate. Whatever degree of mastery they may have over their environment is usually acquired as a result of experience and tradition — which often cease to apply in a new area. The process of removal precipitates extreme mental stress. 'Extreme depression, sometimes even complete mental breakdown and a high incidence of stress-related illness are all common features of the health profile in resettlement areas.'[88]

III. At Work

III.1 Overview

The picture of women in work in South Africa is a changing one. Women constituted 33 per cent of the total workforce by 1980, as compared with 23 per cent in 1960, according to official figures for employment.[1] But while the proportion of women in the workforce is increasing, and while there are shifts in the main sectors in which they work, the effects of the apartheid system are always present *(see Tables VIII and IX)*.

The main sectors in which women work are services (primarily as domestic servants), agriculture and, increasingly, manufacturing. (The official figures for the percentage of the female workforce in these three sectors were 40, 11 and 13 per cent respectively.)[3] For black women, and in particular African women, who are the majority, domestic service and agriculture are the main sectors of work, followed by manufacturing industry. Professional work, mainly teaching and nursing, forms a smaller but significant sector[4] *(see Table VII)*.

A high proportion of those employed in occupations other than agriculture and domestic service are in jobs connected with the world of domestic needs; in food processing or canning works; in garment manufacturing and laundry, and among professional workers, in nursing and teaching. Service categories such as office and shop cleaning, laundry work, cooking, waitressing, tea and kitchen work, as well as messenger service absorb an extremely large number of women. Since the mid-1970s women have moved rapidly into these service jobs. In 1973, 62,468 African women and 21,612 Coloured women were employed in these jobs. By 1981 the figures were, respectively, 112,024 and 32,730.[6]

Official statistics are not accurate. The inadequacy of census figures is compounded by the fact that they cannot encompass women who are working illegally, nor do they include a significant number of women who work in what is called the informal sector — mostly selling small quantities of food and second-hand goods, and doing home sewing.

The number of women working illegally must be high. The difference between the number of men and women working as migrant labourers is stark. The total figure for migrants estimated in 1975 was 1.75m, of which 393,000 were foreign migrants. Of the balance, the figures show:

	From rural bantustan areas	*From other rural areas*
Men	1,030,000	67,000
Women	147,000	113,000

It is believed that the estimated figure of 1.75m amounts to only 80 per cent of the actual migrant workforce. Another 20 per cent of that workforce are illegal migrants. It is safe to assume that the largest proportion of the illegal migrants are women.[7]

Reprisals against those employing illegal workers were increased at the end of 1979 by the imposition of a fine of R500 on the employer. Domestic workers are most affected by this regulation. Whereas in the past an employer would be prepared to turn a blind eye to employing a domestic without the proper permits, a fine of R500 is too much when the employer is paying wages in the vicinity of R360 a year. Those women unable to register and unable to find an employer who will risk the fine, face being abruptly 'endorsed out'. Legislation recently put before Parliament would, if passed, increase the fine to R5,000.[8]

The difficulties of working illegally have been exacerbated partly by these harsher reprisals, and by the constant increase in control over the movements and the lives of all black workers; but also by a dramatic increase in unemployment in the South African economy, which appears to reflect a permanent change. Estimates of unemployment amongst Africans in 1980 ranged from one in four[9] to one in three.[10] South Africa is moving from labour-intensive to more capital-intensive production in both industry and agriculture; money is being invested in machines, and the effects on employment of changing labour processes and methods of production are worse for women than for men. As in other countries, the persistence of the ideology of home-based women conceals both their under-employment and their unemployment.[11]

Women fortunate enough to have legal employment are still confronted with discrimination of various kinds. In this chapter the situation of women, and this means principally African women, working in the main sectors of female employment is described — domestic service, agriculture, manufacturing industry and the professions. This is followed by a section on trends and patterns in the employment of women and in sexual discrimination. The section concludes with a brief look at the role of women in trade union organisation.

III.2 Agricultural Labour

Agricultural work, whether as subsistence farmer or as casual or permanent employee, is one of the main forms of labour for women in South Africa, in particular African women.

59

Women have always been agriculturists in Africa, involved in subsistence agriculture since pre-colonial days, and responsible for most of the agricultural work.

Apartheid in South Africa has distorted traditional village life even more than the intrusion of colonialism in other parts of the continent. It has become impossible to subsist off the land.

Land hunger, the chronically non-arable state of the land, the absence of a large number of men during their economically active years (the men were responsible for the heavy work, hut-building, ploughing), the heavy taxation, the spiralling impoverishment — all these contribute to forcing women off the land in increasing numbers to seek work where they can on white-owned farms.[12]

Women, black and white, make up a quarter of the total full-time farm labourers on farms in the Western Cape. White women are mainly employed by the farmers in a clerical capacity. Coloured women have become full-time farm labourers on the Western Cape fruit and wine farms, replacing the traditional male labour force. On some farms there was in 1983 one man to 12 women. The Western Cape is representative of the whole country in this respect: according to government statistics published in 1984 a quarter of the people employed in the broad category of farm, forestry and fishing workers were women.[13]

Agriculture plays a major role in the economy and, with the exception of gold, this sector brings in more export earnings than any other.[14] It is extremely dependent on hired African labour. Until a few years ago much of this took the form of labour tenancies. The tenants worked for the farmers for part of the year at abysmally low wages, but were able to keep a few livestock and cultivate a small plot of land.

The policy of forced removals coupled with changes in the methods of large-scale farming has been devastating for the labour tenant families as a whole, but particularly so for women. They are not only deprived of access to land, but also of the domestic employment on the farms that supplemented their living. The only skills these women possess are those related to agriculture or domestic service, often not available to them as a legal option because it is increasingly difficult for them to register themselves. More and more farmers are enjoying the extra profitability of migrant, seasonal labour, obviating the necessity of providing housing and land for their workers. Women now constitute the majority of casual workers on farms, often travelling long distances in order to work.[15]

To qualify as migrant workers in 'white' areas, women must register at the local labour bureau; and if, as frequently happens, they are classified as farm workers they will remain so for the rest of their lives, making it impossible for them to find other, better paid employment.

Farm labourers receive extremely low wages. A government survey in 1981 reported an average wage of R25 to R35 in most regions. As in other categories, women are paid lower wages than men. Farmers often prefer to hire women for this reason, and also because they often have to bring with them their children for whom there is no alternative child care, providing the farmer with extra unpaid labour. Because of their inability to get legal work, women are still more susceptible to illegal and low-paid employment.[16]

The wages here at van Heerden's are R20 a month. We have a few cattle that we have raised. But we are not allowed to raise many. Also we are no longer allowed fields. They used to agree. Now? No, no, no. They refused to let us plough but they don't give money. It would be all alright if they gave us a big place to plough and allowed us to have many cattle. Then this R20 of theirs would be alright. Because you would have some maize and some beans, you could sell some. But no, they don't want us to have more than 10 cows.

The whites have money, they have it. Really and truly, they have *lots*. And what can we buy? *Nothing*. They will never, never, never change. We must all get a little strength. All people must have something. If people have no children in Jo'burg what will they eat? We can just die, it's because of this that some of the children swell up and die from hunger. This R20 of theirs is ridiculous. They must know how much sugar costs. There is the same price for everyone who goes to the shop, poor people don't pay less.

We have always suffered on the farms but things were better before. Our parents worked that system of six months without a cent. But they ploughed and they got mealies. Now they have changed. They changed about three years ago. 'The thing of six months is finished. Instead we shall pay money.' Pay how much? Ten rand! If our children go for better work in Jo'burg they will fire us from here. We will have to go to the reserves. That place is terrible, terrible, full and full of stones. Jesus, there is famine there.

I was born on a farm near here. At that place we earned nothing. Yes, and now we are old what will we get? Those boers who used us for free, what will they do for us now that we are old? Nothing.

(A woman speaking in 1982 about life in a white-owned farming area in the Eastern Transvaal — Africa Perspective No. 22, 1983)

Farm workers, like those in domestic service, are not protected by industrial legislation. They lack social security benefits, and they lack bargaining power. The level of wages and the length of the working day are uncontrolled. A study of farm labour in 1982 found that the average hours of work were approximately 60 hours a week spread over 5½ days. Most workers appeared to work a 12-hour day including breaks for meals. But in summer the hours of work sometimes reached 17 hours a day.[17]

III.3 Domestic Work

Domestic service is the largest area of paid employment for women in South Africa. A quarter of all employed women in 1980 were domestic servants, according to the official census nearly three-quarters of a million women. Of these women almost all were black and the bulk (86 per cent) were African.[18]

Domestic workers, states Jacklyn Cock in *Maids and Madams*,[19] are situated at the convergence of three lines along which social inequality is generated: sex, class and racial division. Nowhere else is it possible to find such clear examples of how the racial and sexual factors facilitate and intensify exploitation. The extreme exploitability of women is personified in the domestic servant.

The ideology of a 'woman's place' identifies the domestic sphere of wives and mothers as the 'natural' place for women, and their primary occupation, even if they have other work outside the home. Married women are to be regarded as dependants of their husbands even when economic circumstances have changed the way society operates. Children are identified by the husband's surname, and without it they are 'illegitimate'.

The black domestic servant fulfils the classic female functions of housewife, cook, cleaner, nursemaid, but not in her own home, for the advantage of her husband, or her own children. She cannot even claim the satisfaction of creating a centre of family love and care like housewives in other countries. It is the furthest to which the false concept of 'family' can go, and it is done within the context of the extreme exploitation of black women.

Domestic service is an important part of the economic and racial structures of South African society. Black women perform their roles on two levels, and in a double sense. They remain responsible for the domestic functions within their own households, and at the same time perform these functions within white households. The domestic responsibilities of white women become the responsibilities of the subordinate black women.

Black mothers rear surrogate children. They are separated from their own by the laws of apartheid, while white children have both white and black mothers.

Together with certain other categories (such as agricultural workers) domestic workers are excluded from such protective legislation as does exist.

The Labour Relations Act allows for some organised consultation with employers, but specifically excludes farm workers and domestic workers in private households. The Industrial Conciliation Act, governing relations between employers and employees, wage agreements and conditions, does not apply to domestic workers. Nor does the Wages Act, which recommends minimum wages for various categories.

The Unemployment Insurance Act excludes domestic workers, as well as home workers who are employed for less than one day a week.

The Workmen's Compensation Act excludes domestic workers and casual employees from reimbursement for injury or disease.

None of these acts is particularly effective in championing workers' rights, but the important fact is that the excluded categories are regarded as being marginal to the labour force and have no recourse whatsoever to a limited form of protection.

Many domestic servants live on their employers' premises, another indication that conventional family life is for whites only.

Jacklyn Cock undertook a study of 175 domestic servants and 50 employers in 1978 in an area near Grahamstown in the eastern Cape. The sample is a small one, but the author states that there is no reason to suppose it is unrepresentative.

Almost three-quarters of the full-time domestics earned below R30 a month. The average wage was R22.77. The wages are among the lowest of any in South Africa. The highest wage was R60, earned by only one worker. In 1984 wages for domestic workers in Cape Town were reported as being often between R80 and R125 per month. A meeting of the South African Domestic Workers was told in 1984 that some domestic workers in the Orange Free State were being paid as little as R20 per month.[20]

Of the women in Jacklyn Cock's study 99.9 per cent of domestic workers worked more than a 48-hour week; seven workers in the survey worked more than 80 hours.[21] Almost a third worked a seven-day week; having a day off per week was considered a highly-prized advantage in a job.[22] One mother of three small children was able to visit them once a month on her day off.

Not only did domestic workers work far longer hours than other workers, but they also received less paid leave.[23] The majority had to work on public holidays; a considerable number had no annual holiday. Thirty-four per cent were given one week's holiday a year or less. Less than one-third spent the whole of Christmas day with their families.

All the workers had children. In over half the sample the domestic worker was the sole breadwinner and support for her family.[24] Of the 78 per cent who had been married, only 48 per cent were still married, the others having been widowed, divorced or deserted. The deprivation of family life is severe, and the conditions of life of the domestic worker are an important factor in marriage breakdown. Women who are 'living-in' may not have their husbands stay over even for one night, although the room occupied by the domestic is either separated from the house, or if attached, has a separate entrance. Those who do so illegally run the risk of being caught in police raids on servants' quarters. Even in situations where both husband and wife are domestic workers within the same area, and their respective employers are agreeable, *it is against the law for the couple to live together.* There are no extenuating circumstances, and the vicious operation of the system is illustrated by this letter written by an employer to a newspaper describing a visit of two policemen to a private house:

> The reason for their visit . . . was that we were accommodating an additional African, the maid's three-year old boy, without a licence. The maid explained that the boy normally spent the day with friends while she was at work, but for two days while they were away, she had been forced to bring him with her. He had not slept on the premises and would return each night to the location. This was apparently not legally permitted without the boy having a licence to be with his mother. Under these circumstances my maid was duly fined R10.[25]

To ensure that employers did not close their eyes to the illegal spouse in the back room, a government proclamation made the employer subject to conviction and fine, as well as the employee, should a domestic worker's husband or children be found with her overnight.

Over 50 per cent of the full-time domestic workers in Jacklyn Cock's study began work between 6.00 and 7.00 a.m., a further 43 per cent beginning between 8.00 and 9.00 a.m. Fifty-two per cent stopped work after 5.00 p.m., with close on 20 per cent stopping work after 9.00 p.m. This did not include those nights when the employer entertained. The average work-week was 61 hours.

The long hours make any social life virtually impossible. The women interviewed keenly felt their low status and the image most frequently used to describe their situation was that of slaves — *amakhoboka.*

They are trapped in a condition of subjugation and immobility within which they are subject to intensive exploitation.

The domestic worker does not endorse her subordination but she recognises her powerlessness. In the work place, the disparity in income and lifestyle between worker and employer is highly visible. Black women employed as domestic servants experience apartheid in a peculiarly humiliating way. A black woman looking after a white child at the seaside may take off her shoes and enter the sea to care for the little one, but she is prohibited from bathing there herself. Black women may take their small charges upstairs on the whites' buses, but may not travel on those same buses if not accompanying a white child.

A major part of domestic work in South Africa is washing and ironing, both for full-time servants and for part-time washerwomen. The washerwoman is creating for her employers that 'ideal' domestic environment demanded by whites; the immaculately washed, pressed and folded clothes. In the house, the domestic servant lives daily with a multiplicity of expensive consumer items — furniture, clothes, carpets, electrical appliances, and with the large-scale purchase of food and materials; yet all these must be disassociated in her own mind from any conception of her own needs in her own home. After a day of standing at the ironing board, or fulfilling the multiple functions of a home-maker, she may take her swollen feet to her backyard room, or to the crowded township. But the pleasant home she has helped create belongs to someone else.

White children and many black children learn their places in the structures of apartheid society through the institution of domestic service. White children assimilate racial attitudes through their parents' treatment of black servants — an example constantly demonstrated within the home from babyhood.

For black children, the lessons are different. Lilian Ngoyi, who became president of the Federation of South African Women, described how she was haunted by the memory of going to deliver washing for her mother to a white family, who refused to let her and her baby brother into the house: 'Why should an African child not get into this woman's house, and there is a dog in the house?'

White Women at Home

Black women relieve white women of the monotony and responsibility of domestic work, freeing them to pursue other interests. White women can enrich their lives, economically or socially. They may enter wage employment (34 per cent) mainly as skilled and service workers in commerce and industry. They earn salaries many times as high as that paid to their domestic staff, enabling them to expand their role as consumers.

Most white women in South Africa lead expansive social lives. They are freed from the isolation that marks the mother of young children in the nuclear family of the Western world. They play a lot of sport — bridge, tennis, golf, bowls, swimming. They have many hobbies, largely centring around home and garden, and they entertain frequently. Visitors to South Africa always comment on the free-flowing hospitality they receive, rarely thinking that this is only made possible through the exploitation, economically and socially, of black labour.

But many are unable to utilise their freedom constructively and dissipate it in a round of trivial social activities. After parturition many seem to become redundant, childbirth being the one duty they cannot delegate to the black women. They are not essential for the smooth running of their homes; they delegate the care of their children to the black 'nanny'; and their role as consumer and display of their husbands' wealth become pivotal. The size, grandeur and decoration of shopping centres in the suburbs of large cities bear testimony to this. Many white women, writes Jacklyn Cock, are the victims of a peculiarly dehumanising type of sexual domination.

> The notion of female inferiority and dependence has been deeply internalised by many women. This 'cultural colonisation' renders them open to manipulation in a variety of ways. In the sexist stereotype femininity implies a high level of concern with personal adornment. This is manipulated by the advertising industry to promote endless consumption.[26]

Cock goes on to state that attributes of femininity — helplessness and delicacy — can only apply to a comparatively small number of women resting on the the 'unladylike' activity of others. Olive Schreiner termed this 'the phenomenon of female parasitism':

> Behind the phenomenon of female parasitism has always lain another and yet larger social phenomenon; it has invariably been preceded . . . by the subjugation of large bodies of other human creatures . . . Without slaves or subject classes to perform the crude, physical labours of life and produce superfluous wealth, the parasitism of the female would in the past have been an impossibility.[27]

But some of the freedom from children and home is now being harnessed to combat the threat, increasingly posed as the liberation struggle gathers momentum, on this whole way of life. Already many white housewives are being trained in handling weapons and in concepts of civil defence.

Domestic Workers' Self Image

Viewed from outside, domestic workers appear to be deferential as well as completely powerless. Yet despite their isolation, their work conditions are a form of education; their deference is superficial, a way of coping with their situation, and conceals their true feelings. They have strong perceptions of themselves as women. Only a small proportion of Cock's sample, 16 per cent, thought that women are generally inferior to men in their personal qualities. Many seemed to have a sense of personal superiority to men. The examples cited by Cock include these: 'We are the same, the problem is that we are women. Otherwise I have more power than my husband. Once he gets into difficulties at home, he gives up.' 'We are more capable than men. Men can't face problems. They think it's the end of the world.' 'We are equal but my husband couldn't manage without me.'[28]

Many of those interviewed expressed deep resentment against their wages and their treatment. Cock states:

> Compared to their white, mainly middle-class employers, these women have a much greater 'feminist consciousness' or insight into discriminations against women. The widespread disruption of family life that the system of migrant labour entails, has resulted in the burden of family responsibilities being placed upon black women. Their sense of grievance against what they see as black men's irresponsibility, particularly their drinking habits and secrecy about their incomes, came through very strongly. But their indignation about discrimination against women is clearly overshadowed by their consciousness of discrimination against blacks.[29]

Organisation

In a situation where each worker is isolated, each having to deal separately with a different employer, organisation is a formidable task. However, attempts have been made since 1960, with varying success, to form a domestic workers' union. In 1970, with the assistance of the South African Institute of Race Relations, Domestic Workers and Employers Project (DWEP) was formed. Its chief focus seemed to be organising what were called Centres of Concern where domestics came together on a social basis, and to learn skills. The Domestic Workers Project (DWP) was established by the South African Council of Churches in 1974, expressing the concern that church bodies felt towards the plight of domestics. The South African Domestic Workers Association (SADWA) was launched at the beginning of 1981 as a joint project of the Institute of Race Relations and DWEP. It aims to protect the domestic worker against exploitation, hardship and abuse from employers and officials of the state; to become the mouthpiece of domestics, negotiate with employers and run a complaints office. While the concern of some white women, expressed through their association with the Race Relations Institute and the church organisations, is recognised and appreciated, some black leaders feel the organisations tend to rob the workers of real trade union militancy. The Domestic Workers' Association, representing the majority of black domestics in Cape Town has fought against further legal restrictions on domestic workers.[30]

III.4 Manufacturing Industry

The restrictive laws and practices of apartheid have inhibited movement of black women into industry. The development of secondary industry coincided with the decline in rural output, and these growing industries were increasingly absorbing female labour. In the 1930s and 1940s, however, it was young white women from poor rural Afrikaans homes who came to the towns to service these growing industries, and until 1936 the female workforce in these industries was predominantly white. But the situation was transformed between 1939 and 1946.[31]

As manufacturing industry made even greater strides in the post-war period there was an increased demand for African female labour, which was by far the cheapest. The contradictions within the apartheid framework remained, but for a growing economy African women provided an ideal labour force: women are employed as unskilled labour at the lowest level of production; the wage gap between men and women is as high as 20 per cent, a guarantee of maximum profits; women form a large part of the (industrial) 'reserve army of labour'. Because they form the largest group of unemployed, they are readily available whenever needed in times of expansion, and can be as easily dismissed in times of recession.

The argument that women are paid less than men because they are not the heads of families, and are simply supplementing the family income, does not stand up to scrutiny. In Soweto alone Ellen Hellman estimated in 1971 that one-fifth of the households were female-headed.[32]

Women's legal dependence combined with the impoverishment of the rural areas, migrant labour, and the refusal to recognise African family units all combine to create among African women workers a state of impermanence and insecurity.

African women are paid dismally low wages. In a study carried out by the University of Port Elizabeth in 1982 the average weekly wage of women employed in manufacturing industry was found to be R38, less than half of the absolute minimum required by an average family.[33]

Despite all these restrictions, the extent to which black women are being drawn into employment is one of the most conspicuous features of recent years and the composition of the workforce has undergone steady and continuous change. In 1946, African women were a mere one per cent of the total labour force in manufacturing. By 1950 it was 2.5 per cent, and seven per cent by 1970: by 1979, when women as a whole constituted over 40 per cent of the economically active population (as this is officially defined), African women made up over 20 per cent of the economically active population.[34] Between 1973 and 1981 the percentage of women in the total black workforce (according to official statistics) increased by 7.8 per cent to 22.3 per cent.[35] During the 1960s white women tended to move out of the factories into service occupations such as clerical and secretarial work. African women who were fortunate enough to have relatively secure residential status in the towns began fulfilling the demand for industrial workers, replacing white women in a number of secondary industries, mainly in food, beverages, clothing, textiles and footwear.

Women in industry are concentrated in those sectors related to the concept of 'women's work'. The clothing, textile and food industries together employed 73.1 per cent of all African female production workers in 1970.[36] They are often labour-intensive and for this reason have become targets of government policy to remove them to 'border' areas, or to areas just outside the bantustans ('growth points' is the official term) where there are many unemployed women available, and conditions allow even lower wages than in existing industrial areas (*see below*).

Minimum wage differentiation on the grounds of sex has technically been outlawed but women are generally employed in less well-paid jobs than men. Both the 1956 Industrial Conciliation Act and the 1957 Wage Act endorsed discrimination along sex lines. The Industrial Relations Act of 1982, which is seen as abolishing wage discrimination along sex lines, has done very little to change the situation for African women. The act merely regulates the minimum wages paid to workers, but does not abolish sexual discrimination in practice. Women perform different jobs to men and therefore it can be claimed that they are deserving of different pay.[37]

The working conditions of women in industry are frequently very poor. Because women are employed in labour-intensive sectors, the work is very strenuous. They often have to stand for long hours, only breaking for the lunch hour. Their time is so tightly regulated that a timekeeper may be employed to check on the time they report in and the time spent in toilets.

Employment in industry often means that a woman has to give up her right to have children.[38] In the Industrial Council agreement covering sick leave, no provision is made for maternity leave for female workers who become pregnant, nor special sick leave in the case of pregnant women who suffer miscarriage.[39]

The majority of African women workers are forced to work until the final stages of pregnancy, and undoubtedly many resort to backstreet abortions for fear of losing their jobs. Women in industry have no maternity benefits. The law lays down that a woman be allowed 12 weeks' maternity leave but does not require the employers to keep the job open for women to return after the birth of a child. With unemployment on the increase, such women are very rarely re-employed. If, on the other hand, they are taken back, then their maternity leave is taken as broken service and they suffer a drop in salary. A fair proportion of illegal abortions among blacks are carried out by women who fear that their pregnancy will result in the loss of a job. In some extreme cases, women have opted for sterilisation in order to keep their jobs.[40]

III.5 Border Industries

On the fringes of the bantustans lie border industries, sited either just inside the bantustan perimeter, or close enough to the bantustan to draw labour from it. They are planned as part of the process of keeping Africans out of the 'white' areas while at the same time making the maximum use of the cheapest labour available.

As Prime Minister in 1965, Dr Verwoerd stated: 'White factories on the perimeter of reserved African areas would make full use of tribal African workers, who would thus be absorbed there in the service of white people.'[41]

Industrialists establishing themselves in these areas were offered several inducements, including free removal transportation; financial assistance; a remission of taxes within the first four years; and exemption from some of the provisions of the industrial labour laws — for example, the minimum wage determinations.

Industry was slow to respond to these inducements, and the regime put pressure on light industry to move; and in some instances, large industrial complexes were simply designated to be in border areas, while the neighbouring African townships, established within the urban areas, were reclassified as falling within the bantustan.

The majority of border industries employ women. The wages are not only lower than those that men would get in the same jobs, but lower than those paid in other industrial centres.

The wages are so low that they have in some cases attracted adverse press comment. The area of Babelegi, north of Pretoria and just inside the Boputhatswana bantustan, is the site of a group of such industries. One factory, Kool Look Wigs, with 600 workers, mostly women, paid a basic wage of R4 a week in 1974, an average wage of R6 a week, with no pension fund, no medical assistance, transport or paid sick leave. Four years later when four more Babelegi industries were investigated (three clothing factories and one making tents), it was found that workers were receiving a wage of R6 a week.[42] In 1981, *Grassroots* newspaper revealed that the Frame Group near Durban was employing female migrants from the Transkei because they were willing to accept lower wages than women in the bantustan townships serving Durban. The women were housed in terrible conditions in single-sex hostels and they were required to sleep two to a bed.[43]

Border industries have encouraged the growth of a fringe of sprawling urban slums. They are not towns in any normal sense, as they lack the infrastructural and cultural amenities associated with city life. Moreover, they lack economic viability on their own. They are nothing more than dormitory towns for the border industries, or for commuters who travel further across the border, daily or weekly, or on a longer-term basis. Some workers may travel up to five hours a day — they are lucky to have the work. They are towns in limbo, no longer the responsibility of 'white' South Africa.[44]

III.6 The Informal Sector

There are matters about which it is almost impossible to obtain statistics, and where only rough estimates can be made.

It is not known how many people are deemed by the government to be 'illegally' outside the bantustans. An indication can be gleaned from the fact that, according to the government, 15 per cent of Africans in the Cape Peninsula in 1983 were there 'illegally'.[45]

Who are 'illegals'? They are Africans who do not qualify for urban residence under the pass laws, or who for some reason do not possess the correct documents; who have entered the area illegally; or who are under contract to work on the farms — and therefore not permitted to accept work in any other category.

Since the embargo, imposed in 1969, on women leaving the bantustans except as contract workers, an increasing number of women have been forced by the poverty in the bantustans and the very few opportunities to find work where they live, to become 'illegals'. These women are open to extreme forms of exploitation. Employers are often ready to take advantage of their vulnerable position, especially those women in domestic service.

With the growth of unemployment, women seek survival in what is called the 'informal sector'. This is petty commodity production or trading, involving a wide range of economic activities by which some sort of living is scraped together. By the very nature of the work, the number of people in this sector falls beyond the scope of statistical surveys. With the unemployment crisis in South Africa increasing attention is now

71

being paid to the informal sector which is being brought under stringent control by the authorities.

Beer-brewing and the selling of vegetables are the most common informal occupations among women. With the sale of 'intoxicating liquors' to all Africans prohibited up to 1977, as well as their introduction into the townships, the brewing of beer became a source of sharp conflict between women and local authorities (*see Part IV*).

Over the years the state has made enormous profits from the sale of beer in the state-owned beerhalls. One journalist estimated in 1982 that in the Eastern Cape 'Border' area alone the state sold 50,500 litres of beer a day.[46] Administration Boards (known since 1984 as Development Boards) have been financially heavily dependent on beer profits — a mug of beer contributes towards oppressive control.[47]

Shebeens — illicit liquor 'dens' — became a major part of social life in the townships, and the shebeen queens who ran them were often powerful and commanding women. Although the shebeens were frequently raided, many of the queens had their own arrangements with the police.

In 1980, as part of the much-vaunted 'change in South Africa', the regime decided to legalise shebeens. To operate legally a shebeen owner must have a business licence, the fee for which is R600 a year; and the shebeens should be in owned, not rented, property. Quite clearly these terms eliminate the overwhelming majority of shebeen owners, most of whom will not be able to qualify, and a considerable number of whom do not have Section 10 rights (*see Appendix*), and cannot, therefore, even apply. 'Attempts by the state to control the liquor selling business in areas like Soweto then become part of the strategy to co-opt a black middle class at the same time as ensuring that all those whose stake in the system is limited, are wiped out.'[48]

For women who make a living from selling fruit and vegetables, the situation is only marginally better. Although hawking is not illegal, the authorities have laid down such stringent regulations that few hawkers can comply with them. Hawkers must register with a local authority; must own an approved storeroom; and must move their location not less than a hundred yards at the end of every hour.

Here again, because most women in the informal sector are classifiable as 'illegals', they cannot risk registering with the local authority — that would mean instant expulsion to a bantustan. And moving a stall every hour is another impossible condition.

Women also seek to supplement their incomes in ways connected with domesticity by taking in washing; doing home sewing, mending or making garments; by preparing and selling cooked foods.

III.7 Professions

The position of women in the ranks of professional workers reflects the status of women in South Africa, across the whole spectrum of colour.

Statistics can be misleading. According to the official figures, in 1980 97,300 African women were classified as 'professionals' and only 79,880 men. In fact the African professional men are mainly teachers, and the overwhelming number of black women in the professions are teachers or nurses.[49]

At the university level, only one-third of African students in 1983 were women.[50]

Few of the women in teaching and nursing have the benefit of a higher education.

The high proportion of women teachers is the result of deliberate official policy: 'in order to save money in teacher training and salaries, and also because women are generally better than men in handling small children', stated Dr Verwoerd in 1963.[51] As in all areas of work, women are paid less than men. In 1984 the government introduced new regulations to remove pay discrimination against all women teachers except African women teachers.[52]

The training of nurses could not be subject to the same cuts as that of teachers. Nursing has attracted both white and black women; while the number of nurses doubled between 1946 and 1980 the number of African nurses increased from 3,013 to 21,318.[53] A situation arose in which African nurses were receiving better training than their white counterparts, who were mainly young Afrikaner women. This was at a time when many Africans were still able to receive their preliminary education in mission schools, some with relatively high educational standards, while large numbers of the Afrikaner nurses were receiving a narrow and less competent training from Calvinist institutions in the countryside. Black women were doing better in competitive state examinations, and began to express their resentment against perpetual tutelage by less qualified whites. To protect the white nurses, the Nursing Act of 1957 was passed, prohibiting the employment of black nurses in positions of authority over white nurses.

African nurses and teachers experience immeasurably more taxing conditions of work than their white counterparts, according to Lapchick and Urdang.[54] There are major differences between the facilities provided and what is possible in terms of achievement. For Africans this gap widens once more when rural and urban conditions are compared. Teachers have few facilities and equipment to ease and assist the teaching process. The schools are bare and overcrowded, the writing materials expensive and therefore limited. Their pupils are tired and under-nourished. In contrast white schools enjoy the highest standard of equipment and teaching aids, as well as large playing fields and other amenities. African nurses on the other hand have to battle with illnesses that do not affect the white community, including malnutritional diseases and others aggravated by the conditions of poverty that result from apartheid.

The official Nursing Council was, until 1979, exclusively white. But although black nurses are now represented on it, the majority of the Council remains in white control, and according to black nurses acts to control and discipline them rather than represent their interests.[55]

Among white women a picture prevails that will be familiar to women in many countries of the world. Although they have access to higher education, they are always found on the lower levels of the professions. White males have twice as many Bachelors' degrees, five times as many Masters' degrees and five times as many doctorates as white women, according to 1982 official statistics.[56]

Among white teachers, 65 per cent are women, but women are only 18 per cent of the Inspectors of Education. They are under-represented in important professions. Although white women represent a large percentage of the workforce, they are poorly represented in management: in 1980 only ten per cent of management and senior administrative positions were occupied by women.[57]

A very small number of black women are finding that the changing economic scene is opening gaps for professionally trained women. In recent years some black women of great ability and persistence have succeeded in reaching professional status in various careers; their achievements are exceptional enough to become newspaper stories. The first Coloured woman to become an attorney in the Transvaal was reported in November of 1981. It was 'after a long fight', for attorneys refused to article her. In the 1980s the first black woman to register as a clinical psychologist was reported, and also the breakthrough of another African woman who became a town planner with the West Rand Administration Board.

'They are self-disciplined, independent and hard-working', stated Truida Prekel of the University of South Africa, whose research shows black women entering the professions, industry and white-collar jobs at a faster rate than white women or black men.[58] Their numbers in the professions have doubled since 1969. The actual numbers, however, remain small. For the first time there are black women reaching higher job-levels in the black universities and as technical assistants. Again, this is an indication of 'superficial' progress for these changes can never affect more than a very few. For the majority of women there can never be progress until the whole society moves forward.

III.8 Trends and Patterns of Discrimination

The movement of women into the professions or management is part of a general shift in the distribution of women in various occupations and sectors of the economy. Overall the proportion of women in the workforce has been increasing over the past two decades, more rapidly in some sectors than others. There has also been a shift in the occupational structure and in a number of areas there has been a movement of women into positions that are better paid or of higher status than before.

The shift has however been within the general structure of apartheid. The position of black women relative to white women changes little, and in each sector and within each 'population group' women continue to be disadvantaged relative to men. And the greatest changes, measured in percentage terms, have affected the fewest women: the great bulk of women remain in the lowest paid and most exploited sectors of the economy.

Trends

In the past few years white women have been vacating jobs in the service industries and as clerks and typists to move into higher secretarial and administrative positions, while Coloured, Indian and African women have replaced them. In the 1960s Indian and Coloured women began moving into the clerical and sales sectors and African women into the industrial sector *(see Table VI)*. The bulk of African women, however, have remained in the service and agricultural sectors; in 1981 (50 per cent and 19 per cent respectively)[59] most were migrants on temporary contracts. Eleven per cent of African women were classed by the Department of Statistics as 'professionals', but nurses and poorly trained teachers are part of this category. Nursing and teaching accounted for 94.5 per cent of Coloured women, 86.4 per cent of Indian women and 94.8 per cent of African women who are classed as 'professionals'.[60]

Since the mid-1970s thousands of black women in the towns have been stepping into jobs that were previously only occupied by white women. These are in office work, banking, in the film, hotel and television industries, and most notably in the retail trade, where only a few years ago black sales assistants and cashiers were unknown. Several hotels, according to a press report,[62] have been hiring black women as housekeepers, telex operators and in personnel departments. The banks offer

75

jobs to black women, within the framework of the law which prohibits blacks from supervising whites. The manager of a supermarket group said that 60 per cent of the supermarkets' cashiers in the Transvaal were black women.

Although the number of Africans apprenticed in skilled trades is growing, it is still small. The number of black women in skilled trades is even smaller, but because the wages are low it is also growing, even in areas which have traditionally not employed women.[63]

Where opportunities to move into different jobs do occur, black women are very quick to seize them, as noted above in relation to the professions.[64]

The first black woman to become a clinical psychologist, Connie Pretorius, stated that black women do not feel they have to choose between having children or having a career because of the extended family tradition among blacks. The high value placed on education — often the only thing that black parents can give their children — is one of the causes of black women's growing success in the economic sphere.

The greatest surge forward for black women has come in comparatively new fields such as university professors and technical assistants. Black women make up nearly 70 per cent of all black professionals here.[65]

But still the majority remain in domestic and agricultural jobs, and the fact that the numbers of women in the professions doubled between 1969 and 1982 still leaves the vast majority of black women as unskilled and underpaid.

The upward mobility of women across the colour spectrum is hindered by legal obstacles, by the regime's policy and also by entrenched discriminatory attitudes.

Wage discrimination operates against women in all racial and employment categories, according to the Institute of Labour Relations of the University of South Africa reporting on research done in 1979. White women's wages, though higher than those of other women, were affected by sexual discrimination, with 'more than 80 per cent of the income differentials between the male and female groups due to labour market discrimination against the female'; sexual discrimination against Coloured women represented 75 per cent of the gap between male and female, and Asian women were discriminated against to the extent of 'a mere 28 per cent' of the total. No figures were given for African women.[66]

Education

The movement of women into higher positions in the professions or in commerce and industry rests both on the opening up of such jobs to them and also on there being sufficient women receiving the type of education necessary for such posts. And women's education is yet another area where the lines of racialism and sexism converge.

African people — both men and women — are educated within the system of 'Bantu Education' based on the ideology expressed by Dr Verwoerd in 1954 that there was no place for Africans 'in the European community above the level of certain forms of labour'. The education received by an African therefore, should not mislead him by 'showing him the green pastures of European society in which he is not allowed to graze'.

In this respect, male and female alike suffer the disabilities inflicted by the limitations of Bantu Education.[67] But where women are concerned, government policy is formed not only by the racial imperatives of apartheid society, but by attitudes on the role of women that were imported with colonial society. This in turn becomes a double handicap: the ideology of domesticity with its specific view of women's role separates women from direct participation in economic production or political processes. This ideology is internalised and becomes part of how women see themselves, reinforcing women's subordinate position in society.[68]

The multiple ways in which women are handicapped in seeking education is evident throughout this book. They operate in the home, through parents' attitudes and expectations for their male and female children; in the physiological field, where lack of access to birth control and abortion leads to an extremely high rate of pre-marital pregnancy among African schoolgirls with a resulting high dropout rate. According to one account, 37 per cent of African girls who left school early in 1976 did so because they were pregnant.[69]

Lack of access to education is another important factor, particularly among women in rural areas. Women also have less access to vocational and other institutions. In 1977 there were only 22 schools offering post-primary vocational training for African females; and while vocational training for males included courses related to a variety of industrial roles (building, motor mechanics, electricians and so on), vocational training for girls was limited to dressmaking, domestic science and home management. Stress on domestic skills produces a 'pool of unskilled labour whose talents are untapped'.[70]

The place assigned to women in the social division of labour determines their access to education, and lack of access prevents them from obtaining any but the most rudimentary skills. Illiteracy and inability to speak English and Afrikaans will also hinder rural women in the possibility of obtaining work involving training and skills. In 1980, 49.5 per cent of African women (and the same proportion of African men) had no educational qualifications at all.[71]

III.9 Trade Unions

Despite the many handicaps of women entering industry, the trade union movement has proved to be a training ground for women organisers and political leaders. It was within the trade unions that women first rose to positions of political importance, and the special experience of women as workers has been significant within the resistance movement as a whole.

The trade unions have acted as catalysts for the emergence of effective organisers and leaders in many campaigns against apartheid. They have done this despite tremendous personal cost, for the organisers were persecuted, prosecuted, beaten and harassed, banned and imprisoned, but never defeated.[72]

Historically the leading role taken by women in union organisation was facilitated by the fact that the main law covering labour organisation, the Industrial Conciliation Act, excluded 'pass-bearing natives' from its provisions. Because women were so peripheral to the economy and until the end of the 1950s did not have to carry passes, they were not even defined as 'employees'. This enabled them to play an active role, particularly during the 1940s and 1950s although African trade unions had no official status.

The women trade unionists were so courageous. The government and the employers thought they could be stopped by halting the work of individual women. But the movement was never one of individuals. The spirit of these individual women inspired us whether they were with us or silenced. The government simply does not comprehend the power of the desire for freedom and equality. That power can never be destroyed.
(Bettie du Toit, who has lived in exile after being banned from trade union activity for many years — R Lapchick & S Urdang, 'The Effects of Apartheid on the Employment of Women in South Africa: and a History of the Role of Women in the Trade Union', Paper presented at UN Conference on Women, Copenhagen 14-30 July 1980)

Both black women and white women received a political training through the trade union movement and the process of shop-floor organising. Many of these women who joined the trade unions had not before been involved in politics, but they rose to be leading figures in the liberation movement as a whole.

The women workers' practical experience of the need for unity in labour struggles was carried forward into the women's organisations, giving them their character of non-racialism and acceptance of women from widely divergent backgrounds.

The Industrial Legislation Commission (1950) enforced apartheid by law in the trade unions. In 1954, with the passing of legislation providing for the extension of passes to women, African women were excluded from the definition of employee for the first time under the Industrial Conciliation Act. In 1956, job reservation was enforced by law. Within three years of the Suppression of Communism Act (1950) the government had banned 56 trade union activists, including several women. The government was dismantling the hard-won long-fought-for influence of women in the trade unions. Even in the face of this the women still led strikes, although strikes were illegal.

Last year sometime all the workers at the factory I was working in met and talked about the low wages we were getting. All the workers were women. Everybody talked and we agreed that we should go on strike and demand more money. We were so united nothing could come between us.

On Monday morning we all refused to come in to work but stood outside. Time went by without a single one of us getting inside. The manager quickly phoned the police. Oh! this didn't help him at all. We stayed outside — we knew what we wanted.

The police told us that those who wanted to work should get inside and work. Not a single one of us did go. The owner now sat down to think properly and see what he could do. Then he saw that there was no other solution but to raise our wages.

(A worker describing a strike she took part in during 1982, in a letter to a women's paper — Speak, No. 4, 1982)

By 1960 a generation of women trade unionists whose names had become legendary over the decades of struggle, had been silenced. Amongst them were: Elizabeth Mafekeng, President of the African Food and Canning Workers Union, who was banished far away from her home, her husband and eleven children; Frances Baard, Port Elizabeth Secretary of the Food and Canning Workers Union, who was banished to Mabopane, a thousand miles from her home after spending six years in jail; Mary Moodley, an organiser in the Food and Canning Workers Union, who from the time she was banned in 1963, had only three days in which she was not restricted and silenced until she died in 1979; Bettie du Toit, Secretary of the Laundry Workers Union in the Cape, and Ray Alexander, an organiser in the Food and Canning Workers Union, who were forced into exile.

With a renewed upsurge of strikes among black workers in the 1970s, along with changes in the nature of the workforce needed, and international pressures, the government sought by what they called 'substantial concessions' to bring about co-operation from organised workers. Most trade unionists were not deceived, and workers, both men and women, took great risks in striking in many places. There was a major

79

growth in trade union membership amongst black workers, mainly in new trade unions which were independent of those which accepted the existing official segregated framework of labour relations and trade union registration.

By 1983 there were 24 women general secretaries amongst 240 unions.[73]

Women have continued to participate in trade unions as organisers, secretaries and members who show great solidarity and courage when driven to go on strike. The persecution, bans, arrests and prolonged solitary confinement of these women has not lessened their participation and courage. Women activists have consistently fought for workers' solidarity across the barriers of racialism, sex and class within the trade unions, learning in practice the meaning of unity in struggle; while recognising that their role in the labour front is part of the total struggle against apartheid, for national liberation.

IV. Political Struggle

Makabongwe Amakosikazi — **Honour the Women**

IV.1 A History of Struggle

Just as it is not possible to discuss the problems and disabilities of South African women without discussing the problems and disabilities that apartheid inflicts on the whole black population, so also it is not possible to assess the women's political activities and struggles without surveying the general struggle for liberation.

A historian commented in 1980 on political struggle in South Africa:

> Women in South Africa, from the turn of the century, have emerged as primary catalysts for protest and challengers of the apartheid regime. With all the disabilities and devastating effects of apartheid on the status of women . . . those most oppressed of the oppressed have never lost sight of the fact that meaningful change for women cannot be forthcoming through reform but only through the total destruction of the apartheid system. Thus the common exploitation and oppression of men and women on the basis of colour has led to a combined fight against the system instead of a battle of women against men for 'women's rights'. While women desire their personal liberation, they see that as part of the total liberation movement. Although there is no doubt that the overt leadership has been dominated by men, the seemingly unacknowledged and informal segment of society controlled by women has been the key to many of the most significant mass movements in modern South African history. It is only in the very recent past that the crucial role played by women in raising basic issues, organising and involving the masses has become more widely recognised.[1]

Women's organisations have always operated within the framework of the political resistance movements, because of the women's clear understanding that the reforms they need are dependent upon a restructuring of the state itself. This is one of the reasons that women's participation and initiatives often disappear subsequently from written history. For while it is easy to see the role of women in the political struggle when their activities are specifically among women – as in the various phases of the struggle against the pass laws – it is not as easy to see the pivotal role that they have played in the general activities of the male-led organisations. In various campaigns referred to here, women were not bystanders, nor reluctant participants dragged along by the militancy of the men, but were an integral part of the whole development of the campaigns. Without their activities, the campaigns could not have taken place.

Cherryl Walker[2] comments on the dearth of material on women as reflecting the subordinate position that women have occupied in society, and also the preoccupation of male historians with political and constitutional rather than social history; as well as the historians' own, often unconscious, bias against women, in itself a product of the very social attitudes that reinforce and perpetuate women's subordination within the larger society. For many historians, women are invisible.

Despite their background of a patriarchal society, African women have never occupied the position of subservience that still exists in some parts of Asia and Africa. Even before the traditional pattern had been shattered, women played a notable part in many anti-colonial struggles.

In the innumerable campaigns run by the national liberation movement, although a significant number of women played increasingly important parts, the leadership as a whole has usually been male-dominated, although certainly no more so than we find in countries where women have a longer tradition of political struggle and much greater opportunities.

Dr Fatima Meer[3] writes that Indian and African women in particular have left indelible marks on the modern movement for liberation. 'Indian women at the beginning of the century virtually made Gandhi, and proved the efficiency of the new liberation dialectic of satyagraha that he introduced.' The Indian resistance movement had remained mainly elitist until the women from two ashrams in Natal and the Transvaal transformed it into a mass movement. In 1912 they defied the anti-Asiatic law, crossed the provincial border from both ends and provoked the miners of Newcastle to lay down their picks and strike. A thousand workers then began the epic march led by Gandhi across the Natal border into the Transvaal. According to Meer, 'The great figure of that struggle was not Gandhi, but the emaciated young Valiamma, who refused to surrender despite her fatal illness following repeated imprisonments. She died in the struggle.'[4]

White women of South Africa, except in small numbers, have not generally associated themselves either with the national liberation struggle or with the powerful women's movements. However, it would be wrong to undervalue the work of white women through organisations like the Black Sash and in fields of academic research, while in the

Federation of South African Women (FSAW), the small white membership played a notable role. In the years before the First World War, there were white women suffragettes, inspired by their British sisters, who fought for the right to vote; the right of white women, that is. In those years women, children, lunatics and criminals, together with the majority of black men, were debarred from the vote. White women were not enfranchised until 1930; giving them the vote was partly impelled by the desire to reduce proportionately a small number of black men in the Cape who were entitled to vote.

Passive Resistance and the Defiance Campaign

In 1949, following the return of the Nationalist Party in the (whites only) election, the African National Congress (ANC), benefiting from a new dynamism coming from its Youth League, adopted a Programme of Action calling for strikes, civil disobedience and non-co-operation.

Prior to this the South African Indian Congress, under a more radical leadership than in the past, had in 1946 launched a passive resistance campaign against the Asiatic Land Tenure and Representation Act, aimed at limiting land occupation by the Asian community. Over two thousand Indian resisters went to jail for occupying land that was debarred to them. The Passive Resistance Campaign was of major importance for the political advancement of Indians as a whole, and of Indian women in particular.

Six of the 17 people who initiated the campaign were women, four of them from the Transvaal, who crossed the provincial border into Natal without the necessary permits, and were arrested. Although the actual numbers of women who participated in the campaign were not large (an estimated 300 of the 2,000 arrested were women),[5] the fact of their participation was carried forward into the campaigns run jointly by the Congress organisations in the 1950s and in their participation in the FSAW. A leading figure was Dr Goonam, one of the only five black women medical practitioners in 1946, of whom four were Indian women.[6]

As a first step in the implementation of the Programme of Action adopted by the ANC in 1949, a one-day stoppage of work was called for May Day, 1950. Police fired into crowds of people in the township, killing 18 and wounding 30, including children. The outburst of sorrow and anger that followed the shootings brought together the African National Congress, the Indian Congress and the Communist Party (then about to be declared illegal) in a committee formed to call a national stoppage of work as protest on 26 June 1950. Hundreds of thousands took part in what was primarily a protest against apartheid; schools were empty, shops in the townships and particularly Indian shops in Johannesburg and Durban, were closed. In Port Elizabeth the stoppage was spectacular — all shipping was halted, businesses closed and hotels and garages left without staff. From that time on, 26 June became Freedom Day for South Africa.

The 1950s were turbulent years of political activity. During this whole decade, up to 1960, the emphasis of all the campaign was on peaceful protest, on non-violent methods of struggle. The campaign launched, that of Defiance against Unjust Laws, was a peak in mass action, marked by discipline, humour and determination on the part of the participants. Eight and a half thousand people deliberately courted arrest by defying apartheid regulations and laws, and among those who went to jail was a fair proportion of women. People from all the groups into which apartheid divides the population participated in the campaign.

The liberation movement, now broad-based, having enhanced unity between the different groups, proved itself capable of sophisticated campaigns. It had acquired symbols: a flag, a national anthem, a salute. The women wore a uniform — the black and green blouses that symbolised support for the ANC. The freedom songs composed for each new activity were sung throughout the country.

But each new protest was met by counter-action by the government in the form of new laws that effectively prevented similar protests in the future. Prohibitions and banning orders began to cripple the organisations.

The Congress of the People in June 1955 drew up a Freedom Charter for all South Africans. But it was followed by the arrest of 156 people (16 of them women) on charges of treason (all acquitted after a four-year trial). In 1957 and 1958 there were widespread revolts in many country areas (including those involving the women's anti-pass campaigns described in more detail below). They were met with excessive cruelty, assaults on people and burning of their homes and possessions. On 26 June 1957 there started a campaign of boycott — this, too, became illegal soon afterwards — and the tightening network of new laws and police activity brought ever-increasing repression and brutality.

One of the most horrifying examples of this occurred on 21 March 1960. The Pan-Africanist Congress (PAC), formed in 1959 after a split from the ANC, called a demonstration against the pass laws. At Sharpeville, faced with a large peaceful crowd of protest, the police opened fire. In a bloody scene 69 men and women were killed and more than 180 wounded.

This atrocity was followed by the declaration of a State of Emergency lasting five months. Raids were on a mass scale and hundreds were detained.

The ANC and the PAC were banned. The last legal action taken was the calling of a National Convention by black leaders for May 1961.

The general strike called for 29 May 1961 brought army mobilisation, helicopters and tanks in the townships, and the largest display of naked force brought into play to crush this last, theoretically legal, demonstration against apartheid laws. It was a climax and turning point in political struggle in South Africa. Seven months later the first acts of sabotage took place, with the emergence of Umkhonto we Sizwe, the military wing of the now illegal ANC.

Indefinite detention without trial, solitary confinement and torture brought in an era of political trials.

IV.2 Women's Resistance

Throughout the long years of resistance women played an important part together with men. In addition they initiated and sustained their own protests against apartheid, demonstrating a strength that overcame their greater insecurity and oppression, and the responsibilities of children and homes that often they had to carry singlehandedly.

Because of their comparatively small numbers in industry in the past, black women in general were excluded from the experience in work-solidarity relationships that have often provided a training ground for male political leaders. Domestic servants cannot join together easily to ask for better wages or work conditions; each has to deal individually with a single employer.

Despite the male monopoly of politics, African women burst on the scene in 1913 in a campaign against carrying passes, a struggle that remained a prime objective and proved effective in drawing in mass support.

Although at that time women did not fall within the provisions of the pass laws, local authorities had the power to make byelaws compelling women to obtain permits that in effect were the same as carrying passes — permits that cost them a shilling a month at a time when five pounds a month was an excellent wage.

When petitions and deputations had failed, the women 'threw off their shawls and took the law into their own hands'.[7] In Bloemfontein 600 women marched to the municipal offices and demanded to see the Mayor. When they were told he was out, they deposited a bag containing their passes at the feet of the Deputy Mayor and told him they would buy no more.

Similar demonstrations spread to other towns and many women were arrested and sentenced to various terms of imprisonment. If they were given the option of a fine, they all refused to pay, and officials at small country jails were confronted with the problem of a mass of women prisoners for whom they were not equipped.

Singing hymns, 800 women marched from the location to the Town Hall in the Orange Free State town of Winburg, and told the authorities they were tired of making appeals that bore no fruit, and thus they had resolved to carry no more passes. In a tiny Free State country town this mass demonstration of women was a stupendous event and made a striking impression. But the authorities were adamant and continued to arrest women, who had to be carted from one small town to another to find sufficient jail accommodation.

The struggle continued for years, and eventually these dauntless women were successful. Passes for women were withdrawn.

The same total capacity for defiance and solidarity was to surface among a new generation of women fighting the pass laws in the 1950s.

The earliest political organisation among African women was the Bantu Women's League, formed in 1913 a year after the founding of the ANC. A pioneering woman, Charlotte Maxeke, founded this League, forerunner of the ANC Women's League that would be established 35 years later. Women in the ANC were auxiliary members only, without voting rights until 1943, when they were admitted as full members. At the same conference, the need for a women's league was acknowledged, but it was 1948 before it was officially inaugurated.

The Women's League took some years to build itself into an effective organisation, and in its earlier years the work was largely the supportive type that has always been the women's role: catering for conferences; providing accommodation; fund-raising.

There were many difficulties in stepping outside these limits, comments Cherryl Walker in her book on the history of women's struggles in South Africa.[8] Any form of political organisation against apartheid was difficult. The women's difficulties were compounded by the fact that economically they were more vulnerable, and politically less secure than the men. Patriarchal ideology was deeply entrenched in all strata of society, and both men and women in Congress were conditioned to accept the limitations of the supportive role of the women.

The widening of the scope and the activities of the Women's League came in the 1950s and was a reflection of both the increasing activities and importance of the ANC itself, and also the threat to women of the pass laws.

The organisation that was to play the key role in activating the women against the pass laws was the FSAW (or just 'Womens Fed.') established at a national conference in Johannesburg in 1954. There had been pre-

86

vious attempts to draw women of different groups into one organisation; the Transvaal All-Women's Union was a forerunner of FSAW.

From the beginning, FSAW clearly indicated its double objective of fighting for freedom and liberation for all through the overthrow of apartheid, and of fighting against women's special disabilities. The conference adopted a Charter of Women's Aims, the opening words of which declare: 'our aim of striving for the removal of all laws, regulations, conventions and customs that discriminate against us as women', and went on to declare

> We women do not form a society separate from men. There is only one society, and it is made up of both women and men. As women we share the problems and anxieties of our men, and join hands with them to remove social evils and obstacles to progress.

Thirty years on, women who were not born when the Charter was adopted are reprinting it, finding its aims of emancipating women from the special disabilities suffered by them and of removing all social differences which had the effect of keeping women in a position of inferiority and subordination, as apt and relevant as when the Charter was framed. The FSAW embodied both the idea that women have common interests, and also a strong political attitude.

The FSAW not only linked women's demands firmly with the struggle against apartheid laws, but also fought consistently for trade union rights, and against racial divisions in the trade unions. 'We are women, we are workers, and we stand together.' A number of the leading Federation women were trade union activists.

The first President of the FSAW was a leading member of the Women's League of the ANC — Ida Ntwana; and the secretary was Ray Simons. Later Ida Ntwana resigned and Ray Simons was banned. Lilian Ngoyi was elected president, and Helen Joseph secretary.

The Federation provided for women's organised action on a continuing basis; previously, as in bus boycotts and food committees, it was sporadic.

The Federation was central to the tremendous mass movement among women against passes in the subsequent years; and also thrust to the forefront of the political scene women of exceptional gifts and strong personalities, who not only proved themselves in the women's organisations as able speakers and organisers, but at the same time raised the status of all women within the national liberation movement. The history of the Federation is told in Cherry Walker's book.

In 1955 the then Minister of Native Affairs stated 'African women will be issued with passes as from January 1956'. In fact the law had already been amended in 1950 to enable the regime to introduce passes for women.

Women had reason to fear the carrying of passes, having been forced to witness all their lives the effect of the pass laws on African men: the night raids, being stopped in streets by police vans, searches, jobs lost through arrests, disappearance of men shanghaied to farms, and the prosecutions. It was not even known at the time the degree to which the pass laws would be used to separate family groups and break up homes. But women did know the devastating effect the laws could have on some aspects of their lives. For men, arrest for pass offences could mean loss of job; but for women? They might or might not have a job to lose, but most of them had helpless dependants, often very young babies, who could not be left totally unattended when the mother was whisked off the streets and into jail.

The first big protest against the pass laws organised by the FSAW took place in October 1955 with 2,000 women, mostly African, but including other women, converging in Pretoria, seat of the administration of the Government. The demonstration followed one organised some months before by the Black Sash, white women protesting against pass laws. The black women said, 'The white women did not invite us to their demonstration, but we will invite all women, no matter what race or colour.'

The women's anti-pass movement began to grow. In Durban and Cape Town women marched in their thousands through the streets. The men were amazed at their independence and militancy, but Lilian Ngoyi, one of the leading women, explained:

> Men are born into the system and it is as if it has become a life tradition that they carry passes. We as women have seen the treatment our men have — when they leave home in the morning you are not sure if they will come back. If the husband is to be arrested, and the mother, what about the child?[9]

The regime began the issue of passes by selecting sections of the women least likely or able to protest: farmers brought lorry-loads of women workers from their farms to get their passes and the women knew what would happen if they refused. Even these country women would sometimes subsequently burn their passes as protests grew all over the country, culminating in a mass demonstration in Pretoria, one year after the first one, on 9 August 1956 — the day that has since been designated 'Women's Day' by the liberation movement in South Africa.

A year before it had been 2,000 women. Now 20,000 women assembled, overcoming tremendous difficulties imposed both by their personal positions and by the authorities, to join the assembly. Despite the most ingenious forms of intimidation the women saved and worked together to raise money to hire trains, buses, cars, to bring them thousands of miles to the capital. All processions in Pretoria were banned that day, so the women walked to Union Buildings to see the Prime Minister in groups of never more than three. All Pretoria was filled with women. This was four years before the national liberation organisations were banned, and thousands of women wore the green and black Congress blouses; Indian women dressed in brilliant saris; Xhosa women in their ochre robes with elaborate headscarves.

They arrived in trains, on buses, by cars and on foot and gathered in the amphitheatre of the Union Buildings. Each woman had signed a petition protesting against the new pass laws. Nine leaders, representing women of all groups in South Africa, carried the piles of petitions to the Union Buildings in search of the Prime Minister, Mr J G Strijdom. They were stopped by a commissionaire who eventually let five of them through. Among these five were the late Mrs Lilian Ngoyi, then president of the Women's League of the now banned ANC and Mrs Helen Joseph (the first woman to be placed under house arrest).

When they were told the PM could not see them, they left the petitions at his door and returned to the other women. We were so angry, very, very angry. We had written to him for an audience. He was expecting us. But he was not there. Earlier a helicopter arrived at the back of the Union Buildings. We think he fled from us on that.

He had so much power, but he was scared of us and all we had done was to come peacefully and tell him that we, the women of SA, said "No" to passes. The women then stood in silence for 30 minutes as a sign of protest. The only noise in the whole amphitheatre was the cry of babies. Then we went home and organised in our communities.

The women opposed the passes because it meant that homes would be broken up and mothers separated from children when women were arrested under pass laws; that women and young girls would be exposed to humiliation and degradation at the hands of pass-searching policemen; and that women would lose their right to move freely from one place to another. We have seen all this come true and it continues to happen. Look at KTC and Crossroads. Everyday the black people suffer because of pass laws.

(Dorothy Zihlangu, a member of the United Women's Organisation in the Cape, recalled the 1956 demonstration — Argus 8.8.84)

Union Buildings is designed in classic style, with pillared wings on either side of an amphitheatre on a hillside, with trees and gardens in steps down the hillside and a vista to the town far down below a long avenue of lawn. The women slowly converged up this avenue and filled the amphitheatre. Their leaders went into Union Buildings and left hundreds of thousands of signatures on petition forms at the office of the Prime Minister who, of course, was not available to see them. Afterwards they stood in complete silence in the winter sun for thirty minutes, then burst into magnificent harmony to sing the anthems, *Nkosi Sikelel' iAfrika* and *Morena Boloka*. The singing, as they dispersed, echoed over the city, and the women began a new freedom song with its refrain *'Wathint' abafazi, wathint' imbokodo, uzokufa'* — 'now you have touched the women you have struck a rock, you have dislodged a boulder, you will be crushed'.

The protests continued, but so did the issue of passes. The authorities made it inevitable. Old women who went to collect their tiny pensions were told 'No pass book — no pension'. Mothers could not obtain the registration of the birth of a child unless they had their passbook. Teachers and nurses were dismissed if they refused to take passes. Gradually more and more women were forced to accept them.

Not only did the more sophisticated women of the towns organise in protest. Remote country districts were involved, and the struggle was most bitter in the area of Zeerust in the Western Transvaal. There, the issue of pass books fused with deep opposition to the Bantu Authorities Act that was being implemented in the district. The Act incorporated the office of chief of the tribe into the hierarchy of government, making him virtually a civil servant. When the issue of passes began, many women accepted them, but others refused. In one village only 76 out of 4,000 women accepted books. The Government arbitrarily removed the chief, who sympathised with the women, and replaced him with their own appointee who was supported by a gang of strongarm thugs. The revolt against the passes became involved with the opposition to the stooge chief, and to the changes in laws brought by Bantu Authorities. The women's resistance became open confrontation. Women who had accepted the passes burnt them. Those who had not yet taken passes refused to do so.

The displays of militancy by traditionally subordinate women had a profound effect on men — white as well as black, comments Joanne Yawitch.[10]

> Action by women was fundamental. For women are conceptualised as being the centre of stability and security. The arrest of the women radicalised the men, and in the case of the white men, rioting by African women was perceived as a threat to the entire social structure and to all order.

Dr W M Eiselen, secretary for Bantu Administration and Development, stated that:

> Recognition of the women's demonstrations on the lines that have found favour among the whites, that is, where women

already have a status altogether different to that of Bantu women, can at this stage only have a harmful and dangerous effect which can undermine the entire community structure.[11]

Action against the women was taken under the direction of a police sergeant, van Rooyen, who was a gross and sadistic man. Under his direction, utilising the new chief's strong-arm men, a terrible punishment was exacted from the people. Some were shot, many more beaten, their homes burned to the ground and all their possessions destroyed.

The women in the first group were slashed raw. They said that 23 other women were similarly injured 'but we do not know where they have run'. Injuries were distributed mainly about their arms, backs and shoulders, but their faces, breasts and bellies and thighs had suffered too. The standard injury was a sort of gash of varied length. Clothes clotted with blood adhered to the wounds.[12]

The wounds had been inflicted by bodyguards of the government's stooge chiefs, with strips cut from tyres and sharpened at one side like a knife.

Mrs Makgoro Maletsoe, who burned her pass book, was sent to jail and on release crept quietly back to her village at Witkleigat. She knew the chief's thugs were beating up those who had resisted the pass laws. On her return, she saw another group of women being arrested, and among them a friend who she knew had an unweaned infant. Makgoro Maletsoe ran to her friend's hut and fetched the baby, which she handed to its mother before she was taken away. This aroused the bodyguard who surrounded the women and then attacked them with clubs. The group were then cast into a hut where they spent the night, 'Mrs. Maletsoe hovering between an agonizing wakefulness and insensibility. She had entirely lost the use of her right arm, and her face and body were smashed and torn.'

These women were not charged with any crime. The next morning the regular police came, brandishing guns, but eventually set them free.

By devious routes, despairing friends managed to get Makgoro Maletsoe out of the sprawling village, into a car, and away to Johannesburg . . . for a month she lay in a hospital bed. Besides the injuries inflicted on her face and torso by boots and kieries [clubs], her right arm was broken in three places.

When she was well enough, she laid a charge of assault. The Attorney-General declined to prosecute.

This was the price of political struggle for women in South Africa. More than two thousand women and children fled from the persecution over the border into Bechuanaland (now Botswana) where the women did not have to accept passes. Individuals were sent into banishment, others went into hiding for months on end. The police units had wide powers of search and arrest, and sealed off the area so that reports of what was happening filtered out with difficulty.

But even in this atmosphere of force and terror, the women still resisted. At times they even taunted the police, as the incidents below illustrate.

Police who arrived in a country village in 1957 to arrest about 20 women who had burned their pass-books, found 200 women patiently sitting together under the trees.[13] The sergeant demanded the women for whom he had come. 'We are here', the women replied.

He asked them to step forward. 'If you arrest one, you must arrest us all', they said.

The sergeant had to hire railway buses to transport the women to jail; their number had increased to 233. They filled the yard of the police station — singing. Food had to be provided; the jail could not cope with them, nor the sanitation. When they were told they were being released, the women demanded buses to take them home. The crowd of arrested women had unaccountably increased from 233 to 400.

The women formed a procession around the sergeant and his aides, singing a new song with many verses, and the refrain:

> Behold us joyful,
> The women of Africa,
> In the presence of our BAAS:
> The great one
> Who conquers Lefurutse
> With his knobkerrie,
> And his assegai,
> And his gun.

On another occasion, in July 1957, in Gopane Village in the Baphurutse Reserve, some women burned their passes. When 35 women were arrested, 233 more volunteered to be arrested. When officials arrived in Motswedi and Braklaagte to register the women, the villages were deserted. In June, 1957, at Pietersburg in the Northern Transvaal, 2,000 women stoned officials who came to register them. When the officials returned in July, 3,000 women greeted them, again forcing their withdrawal.

The dominant part played by women in these campaigns was due to various factors, one being the absence of so many of the migratory males, so that a large part of the rural population was female. The men's absence also increased the burden of responsibility on the women, and the women bore the brunt of the new legislation. While seeing the women as subordinate and inferior, the authorities were keenly aware of the women's action as a fundamental threat to their authority. Eiselen declared:

> Officials of the department have been instructed not to have discussions with the masses of women and their so-called leaders, but to make it clear to them that they will always be willing to have discussions with the recognised bantu authorities, the tribal chiefs and responsible male members of the community.[14]

In an account of women's protests in 1959 in rural areas of Natal, Joanne Yawitch[15] relates how in October 1959 in Ixopo, 500 women from surrounding districts marched to the town demanding to see the Native Commissioner for a reply to grievances they had submitted two months earlier. Dr Margaret Mncadi, a woman's leader who commanded great respect, organised this march.

The Native Commissioner's response was to tell the women to return home and give their demands to their husbands who could then take them to the local headman, and in this way official (masculine) channels could be followed until the message was relayed to him. The women refused to disperse until they could speak to a 'Native Women's' Commissioner, and their strategy of going down on their knees in prayer when told to disperse resulted in arrests, with fines or imprisonment.[16] The exact number of women involved in the Natal rural unrest is not known, but Yawitch quotes the figure of 20,000 women, with nearly a thousand being convicted on various charges. The women were responding to threats by the authorities to what they saw as traditional roles, and also to their traditional economic function in the brewing of beer.

The authorities refused to listen to the women because to do so would have meant not only accepting their grievances, but also accepting women on an equal basis with men — an acceptance that threatened fundamental social and political assumptions.[17] In these ways the revolt of the women in the countryside had a significance beyond the immediate issues that ignited them.

The officials failed to see the extent to which women were being driven by the currents of economic change. The war years brought industrial growth demanding a constant supply of labour. The stagnant bantustans were now increasingly under pressures that accelerated the crumbling of their economic and social order. Not only could they no longer give even limited support to their populations, the conventions on which their inhabitants' lives rested were also disintegrating as the customs that had sustained them became increasingly irrelevant to the women's lives. Not only irrelevant, but in their distorted forms, a barrier to any improvement.

IV.3 Boycotts

The conditions in the urban areas, where industry had caused a dramatic increase in population, were made more tolerable by the neglect of essential housing and other needs during the years of the 1939-45 war. War brought inflation, a rising cost of living, periodic food shortages and, most of all, an acute housing shortage. All these are areas where the burden is felt most keenly and personally by the women, and in all these areas the women became increasingly active. In the 1940s food committees were formed in Cape Town and Johannesburg, and also co-operative food clubs in working-class areas for the purchase and distribution of vegetables, and with the aim of forcing local authorities to open suburban markets.

The organising of food purchases at the wholesale markets, the sorting, pricing, distribution in the co-operatives; the direct attacks on food hoarders, the organising of deputations to local authorities and other protests — all these activities were training schools for women.

In 1943, 15,000 men and women walked 18 miles a day for nine days in protest against a one penny rise in bus fares. They lived in Alexandra Township, nine miles outside Johannesburg, and worked in the city. In mid-winter, in the sharp cold of the highveld, domestic servants and washerwomen with heavy loads of clothes on their heads marched together with factory and shop workers from early morning when it was still dark until late at night. A year later there was a second boycott, this time lasting seven weeks. More men than women work in the city, and therefore more men marched. But the participation of the women was significant. Women who were not working in the city stationed themselves at the bus terminus in Alexandra to make sure that no young men weakened in resolve and entered the buses that were lined up and waiting for passengers.

Particularly during the long second boycott, some middle-class white women drove their cars to and from Alexandra in the mornings and evenings, specifically to give lifts to women, where possible to the older women who obviously suffered from the long march.

The drivers were stopped by the police, who charged them with carrying passengers without a permit. These white women encountered for the first time in their lives the sharp edge of opposition to authority, and the abysmal poverty and hardship of the lives of the black women. Their action was a gesture of solidarity with other women, transcending the formidable barriers of apartheid.

The huge influx into black townships reached bursting point in 1944 when, in the words of one of their leaders, 'the people overflowed'. A series of squatters' movements began, in which families who had been living as sub-tenants in small houses already overcrowded, set up their own shacks in shanty towns on the hillsides outside the black township of what was then known as Orlando (today incorporated into the whole complex called Soweto). Men were in the leadership of these movements, but without the commitment of the women they could never have taken place. Corrugated iron — where it could be obtained, flattened tins, cardboard and sacking were the building materials in the shantytowns. Within these homes, women cared for the family, fed the babies, cooked for the children and the men, washed clothes in basins among the earth and rocks, confined day and night against the sacking of the shacks around them. The men had some relief; they went to their jobs in the city. Whether in paid employment, or not, the women had the burden of their 'housework' and their responsibilities to their families.

On many occasions the municipal authorities sent officials during the day with new orders and demands on the women. On one occasion, they tore down a whole section of shanties, piled wood, sacking and other materials on to a lorry (where they 'caught fire' and burned). The women and children huddled into the grounds of a church, trying to erect some protection for their children when it began to rain. It was only the toughness and determination of the women that kept these mass movements going. Nearly two decades later, they are again setting up their homes in shacks, and again having them destroyed.

The participation of women was also a key factor in the campaign in 1955 against the introduction of 'Bantu Education' (see Appendix). As a protest against this inferior form of education for Africans the Congress movement organised schools in the townships in which white women also participated; in almost all of these the teachers were women. The regime made it illegal to teach children (or adults) at unregistered schools. The township schools became 'cultural clubs'. Inspectors were sent round to the clubs, many of which were held in the open air, and if there were any school materials — books, slates, pencils — the teacher would be arrested and charged. In court cases the evidence handed in would be a blackboard and chalk, or slates, and the claim that the woman in charge was actually trying to teach the children to read or do sums. To circumvent this, the teachers devised rhymes and games that would teach numbers and letters, and used a pointed stick to write in the dusty sand, so that it could be instantly obliterated if the police arrived.

Of course, the Congress movement had not the resources to provide a proper system of education as an alternative to the bantu education of the State, but while these schools lasted they were an effective form of protest against one of the most pernicious features of apartheid.

Women's deep resentment against municipal beerhalls was another source of demonstrations and clashes with the police that flared up from time to time in many different urban townships.

The issue was not a simple one. The brewing of a beer with a low alcoholic content was traditional, the serving and drinking of the beer being closely bound up with tribal ceremonies and customs. The women wished to continue their home-brewing when they came to the towns, and in addition, it was an important source of supplementary income for them. But up to 1977 the laws prohibited not only the sale of 'intoxicating liquors' to all Africans, but also their introduction into the townships. The local authorities opened beerhalls where men could go to drink municipally-brewed beer in bleak surroundings, but could not take it home. For thirty years the issue of home-brewing had fuelled women's oppositions to local authorities. Beer boycotts were perennial and vigourously pursued. In 1945 in Springs, on the Witwatersrand, police fired on women who were demonstrating, and assaulted many of them. Later 111 Africans appeared in court, the majority women. In 1949 in Krugersdorp a beerhall was destroyed by fire during protest riots. There were many more incidents in which the beerhalls were the targets.

The black township of Cato Manor in Durban was the centre of large-scale protests. It was an area of shacks; the women complained that the administration provided no lights and no sewerage; that their husbands' wages were grossly inadequate; that the police constantly raided their homes at night. Protests began to centre around the beerhalls and, in June 1959, discontent exploded when 2,000 women marched to express their multiple grievances. The police, loathed both for their own behaviour and as instruments of oppressive laws, charged the women with batons, striking them to the ground, even hitting the babies tied to their backs.

IV.4 A Legacy of Hope and Defiance

By 1958 passes were being issued in the major centres, and although there was still resistance, it had become isolated and fragmented. Towards the end of 1958, the 'reference book' units finally reached Johannesburg and began to issue passes cautiously, at first to those sections of women least able to refuse. But women in the ANC Women's League reacted with fierce resistance in a campaign of civil disobedience. Women who marched to local Native Commissioners' offices in protest were arrested for holding illegal processions: 249 the first day, 584 the next, and by the end of the week 934. The following Monday another 900 women were added to those already crowding the cells in central Johannesburg. 'The prisons and police stations of Johannesburg were in an uproar, their facilities stretched to breaking point with the enormous intake of women.'[18]

The arrests were splashed across the newspapers. The black magazine *Drum* said it seemed like a festival, with the defiant women singing and dancing. The Johannesburg *Star* headlined its report 'No Nannies Today' — a crisp statement of how most white South Africans viewed African women.[19]

Although the demonstrations had arisen almost spontaneously, once they had begun both the ANC Women's League and the FSAW gave wholehearted support to the women. Impressed by the militancy and discipline of the women, they wanted to adopt a policy of 'no bail and no fines' for those already in jail, while maintaining outside support.

Helen Joseph recalled the situation:

> Their attitude was they're not going to accept passes. That's when the first mass arrest took place . . . Within the space of a week there were 2,000 women in jail. It was incredible. [They] left their children, left their husbands, left their homes, went to jail and simply would not pay the fines.

> The men felt they couldn't cope with the home situation any more. All they had to do was to go up to the jail and pay the fine,. And if you're in jail and your fine is paid, you're put out. The women were very angry but they couldn't do anything about it.

The campaign was discontinued and superseded by a general anti-pass campaign. The deeply-felt opposition of the women to passes had not lessened, but the overwhelming authority of the state and the many different tactics used to make women accept them gradually broke down resistance.

> We have to carry passes which we abhor because we cannot have houses without them, we cannot work without them, we are endorsed out of towns without them, we cannot register births without them, we are not even expected to die without them.[20]

The Sharpeville massacre marked the end of an era of non-violent protests, and a new, more repressive time began in March 1960 and with the subsequent banning of the ANC and PAC.

A proclamation was issued in October 1962, making it obligatory for women to carry passes as of February 1963, and by that time, the FSAW had been virtually silenced and driven underground.

It had taken the government 11 years to impose its pass legislation (first passed in 1952) on the women of South Africa. The courage, the discipline, the unity of women had been demonstrated over and over again. The issue of passes for women was fundamental to apartheid policy, it had to be imposed if the bantustan strategy was to be inaugurated. The women had to be contained. But the inspiration of their prolonged fight and the deeper understanding it produced were passed on.

'Among us Africans', stated former ANC President and Nobel Peace Prize winner Albert Lutuli,

> the weight of resistance has been greatly increased in the last few years by the emergence of our women. It may even be true that, had the women hung back, resistance would still have been faltering and uncertain . . . The demonstration made a great impact and gave strong impetus . . . Furthermore, women of all races have had far less hesitation than men in making common cause about things basic to them.[21]

In her summing up of the FSAW's achievements, Walker describes it as a political organisation that broke new ground for the women of South Africa, three main aspects of its programme being its commitment to the emancipation of women, its commitment to the national liberation movement and its non-racialism. Its rejection of colour-consciousness that had permeated other women's organisations was strengthened by its more developed feminist consciousness. Because women were seen to suffer serious disabilities on account of their sex, the FSAW could envisage the possibility of a universal women's movement aimed at removing those disabilities and cutting across existing colour lines. The legacy it has left is one of 'an open-hearted belief' in a free and non-racial society, a legacy of hope and courage.[22] Helen Joseph described the legacy of the FSAW as one of self-confidence, for none of the women had any doubts about the ultimate future; 'I think we inherited a legacy of hope and defiance, and passed it on.'[23]

In September 1959, at a special conference convened by the ANC — the last before it was banned — a bright red banner proclaimed: MAKABONGWE AMAKOSIKAZI — Honour the women.

IV.5 The Struggle Continues

From the 1960s onwards laws of increasing harshness were matched by accelerating ruthlessness in the police and security forces. Many women as well as men have suffered prolonged solitary confinement, indefinite detention without trial, torture and years of imprisonment. Some were detained to try to make them give evidence against others; or simply because the police thought they might have some 'information'. Some were directly involved in activities that led to arrest and political trials. Many more have been affected by the long and often uncertain imprisonment of husbands, sons, fathers and friends.

Women have been prosecuted on a wide variety of political charges reflecting the range of their involvement in the struggle against apartheid; including treason, 'terrorism', sabotage, membership of or assistance to a banned organisation, helping people to escape from the country, recruiting guerillas, breaches of banning orders and similar charges. Among those who are serving or have served jail sentences are women of all colours, ages and religions. There are young girls, many mothers, and grandmothers, some over 70 years old.

Some of the cruellest punishment is administered without any charge or trial, simply for outspoken opposition to apartheid. Many women have suffered indefinite detention without trial, in solitary confinement; have been subjected to torture during interrogation; served with crippling restrictions; put under house arrest; placed under extensive bans on their activities.

For many women in prison the punishment is compounded by separation from their children and uncertainty about their fate. When Jane Ntsatha appeared in court in August 1982 charged with recruiting members for the ANC, she highlighted a problem which may be faced by women political prisoners, for with her in the dock was her 16-month-old son, Mayibuye. The child had been detained with his mother the previous November, and had spent most of his life behind bars. The presiding magistrate refused to let the trial commence until a woman in the public gallery offered to look after the child.

When Khosi Mbatha and her husband Alex were both detained in 1981, their youngest child, three-year-old Dudu, was taken into custody with them. They were told 'The child is also a terrorist and communist so she must go to gaol.' Two days later mother and child were forcibly separated. Khosi was told her daughter had been taken to a reformatory. In fact the child was dumped outside their house by security police, and was only later rescued by friends.

Two women political prisoners, Montshidisi Serokolo and Thandi Modise, were pregnant at the time of their arrest in 1978 and 1979 respectively. Thandi had left South Africa after the Soweto uprisings, intending to study abroad, but instead she underwent military training and had been on active service within South Africa for 18 months before her arrest. At her trial she related how she had been repeatedly assaulted by three policemen during her pregnancy. She is serving eight years' imprisonment and her daughter is being cared for by relatives.

Rita Ndzanga had to leave four young children when she and her husband were both arrested in 1969, and with others became the victims of a prolonged police operation of solitary confinement, trial, discharge, re-arrest, a second trial; during which period she suffered the torture of repeated assaults and sleeplessness. When the second trial collapsed she was released, but later she and her husband were both arrested, and he died at the hands of the security police. Both before these events, and afterwards in the 1970s, she was placed under five-year banning orders.

. . . **They would come in the middle of the night. The last key in the succession of prison doors belongs to security police — all other doors can be opened by prison staff.**

So they would come at night. I couldn't sleep flat by then I had to elevate myself with the few blankets I had. You just heard someone interfering with your neck, they came with a wire. He says I'm going to strangle you, because you don't want to tell the truth or tell me about other people. I will tell the whole world that you've committed suicide. Then he'd walk out.

Some days I'd feel cold steel next to my temple. He would say I'm going to shoot you and nobody will ever know about you because I've got the power, the privilege, and the protection, as a policeman. Then he walks out, just like that.

Some days they would come in and beat me up in the cells . . .

(Khosi Mbatha, at a press conference in London in November 1982, speaking about her detention in 1981)

Despite all this, Rita Ndzanga remained an active trade unionist. In June 1984 she was once again in detention, under Section 29 of the Internal Security Act, which allows no access or contact with a lawyer. She was detained for four months. At the time of her arrest she was treasurer of the General and Allied Workers' Union and Transvaal treasurer of the United Democratic Front (UDF).

Joyce Dipale, after leaving South Africa, described how she was kept in solitary confinement in 1976 and 1977 for 500 days under terrible conditions. She was subject to many agonising forms of torture, including the 'horse' — she was handcuffed to a pole and swung round and round until she lost consciousness — electric shocks on her bare breasts, buttocks and genitals ('I got used to the pain, but never the humiliation'); beatings; prolonged standing with deprivation of sleep, food and water; and being kept in a dark room, she does not know for how long — 'I lost touch with time'.

Shanthie Naidoo, held in solitary confinement in 1969 with the intention that she should be forced to give evidence at a political trial, refused, and was sent to jail for two months. In court she gave a graphic account of the effects of interrogation coupled with prolonged sleeplessness. She stood for five days and five nights, interrogated all the time by relays of police. 'I lost track of time and for periods my mind went blank.' At one stage, during such a blackout, she dreamed she was being interrogated, and answered questions in her sleep.

Lilian Keagile was 25 when she was detained in November 1981. After eight months in solitary confinement, she was brought to court and charged with furthering the aims of the ANC. She gave evidence of beatings, choking with a wet sack, and sexual assault. Her cousin, Ernest Dipale, who was to have been her co-accused died in the hands of the police.

Dorothy Nyembe, a leading activist and organiser for the Women's League and the FSAW served her full sentence of 15 years for 'harbouring guerillas'. She was released in 1984. A tireless organiser, who took the lead in many struggles in Natal, she kept her spirit of defiance during 15 long years, fighting for better conditions in prison and going on hunger strike. She emerged unbroken, as strong in her determination as when she defied unjust laws in 1952.

Information on the conditions and treatment of women political prisoners is scarce, but the experiences of individual women prisoners indicate that their conditions may in some respects be even harsher than those endured by male political prisoners. Their isolation from the outside world is accentuated by the difficulties and obstruction which relatives face in locating and visiting them in prison. Dorothy Nyembe, released after 15 years' imprisonment in March 1984, said that she was not allowed to study throughout her sentence. Newspapers were denied to all the women prisoners in the prison where she was held for the final years of her sentence. Nyembe also said that while she was initially held in Barberton Prison, visits from her family were forbidden and letters at first did not reach her, because they were not written in English.

Five women political prisoners gave evidence in court of their harsh treatment. Caesarina Makhoere, serving five years, was held in solitary confinement for two and a half years from April 1979 to October 1981 after she had participated in a hunger strike. During the whole of this time she saw no one except prison officials, save for one ten-minute visit from her mother. Another of these prisoners, Elizabeth Gumede, 60 years old and suffering from hypertension, found her isolation so claustrophobic that she screamed for long periods. Eventually, in October 1981, the five women submitted an application against the Minister of Justice to have their detention in isolation declared illegal. They reported how they had little exercise, were refused all reading matter except the Bible, and were allowed few letters or visitors. Their appeal was dismissed.[24]

Barbara Hogan, sentenced to ten years' imprisonment for treason in 1982, brought an action against the officer commanding the new Johannesburg Prison and the Commissioner of Prisons, stating she was being maltreated by prison staff and 'may not survive mentally and physically the cruel and inhuman treatment'. She said certain rights and privileges were being denied her, complaining that she was kept in isolation, frequently denied exercise and that letters and visits were withheld. She also said she had had difficulty getting study materials.[25]

Women serving long sentences face years separated from their children, and in many cases are also deprived of news of them. For others, a long sentence may rule out the possibility of motherhood.

There are many more women who are the dependants of men political prisoners. The conviction and imprisonment of the man often leads to the endorsing out of town of his family, who may lose the right to live in a township outside a bantustan and are sent to resettlement camps. Many young women — eldest daughters — are left to cope with families of small children when both parents are arrested; frequently it is the grandmothers who carry the burden.

Thus the participation of women in the political struggle in South Africa is not confined simply to those who are directly involved, but spreads to encompass wives, mothers and grandmothers throughout the country. Often they are left alone to contend with all the problems of poverty, work and child-rearing with the additional problems of homelessness, expulsion to the bantustans and all the distortions of life that these impose.

IV.6 Soweto and After

Soweto

In June 1976 a demonstration of schoolpupils protesting against the enforced use of Afrikaans in their schools began a chain of events that rapidly became a national uprising of schoolpupils against apartheid.

It is not necessary here to describe the heroic and tragic events that started in Soweto and spread to towns and townships throughout South Africa, but simply to record that girls and women were involved in all phases of the uprising.

This was seen in the photographs of the students on their protest marches, with girls in their old-fashioned gym-slips well to the fore; in the number of women held as detainees under the new Internal Security Act; and in the grim evidence of the mortuaries, where parents sought the bodies of their daughters as well as of their sons.

One morning I decided I also had to participate, I also had a part to play — and I joined the crowd . . . there had already been lots of killings, and the children were playing in the streets, when suddenly a police van passed, a seven-year-old child raised his fist and said 'POWER' — whereupon the policeman got off the van and aimed at the child and shot at him directly . . . When the police started to shoot that is when students picked up stones, hit back, and took dustbin lids to protect themselves . . .

(Sikose Mji, speaking about events in June 1976 — 'The Role of Women in the Struggle for Liberation in Zimbabwe, Namibia and South Africa', Paper prepared for UN Conference on Women, Copenhagen, 14-30 July 1980)

It was a black woman journalist, Sophie Tema, who gave the world the first eyewitness account of the initial police massacre of the children. And during the three days and nights of unrelieved horror that followed, as well as during subsequent weeks while clashes continued, it was a group of women members of the Black Women's Federation, who organised in the most practical way possible. They went into the thick of the fighting to try to help families. As they drove round the township, groups of children told them where they would find the dead and the injured. These women went into a nightmare of smoke and shooting to help other women find their children, often dead or hideously wounded, sometimes blinded or paralysed by gunshot.

Even initially, during the peaceful demonstrations, parents supported the pupils. But what really thrust the parents into action was the brutal police killings . . . Nobody expected the cold-blooded murder of young children. So besides their solidarity with young people they were angered — and their hatred and rejection of the whole system came to the surface. They were completely with the students in their militancy.

(Nkosazana Dlamini, formerly Vice-President of SASO, speaking of the events of June 1976 — Southern Africa (New York), March 1977)

Among those identified as 'agitators' and flung into detention as the upsurge continued were a number of well-known women: Winnie Mandela — once again; Dr Fatima Meer, a sociologist and first president of the Black Women's Federation; Joyce Seroke of the South African Young Women's Christian Association; Sally Motlana, vice-president of the South African Council of Churches; Dr Mamphela Ramphele, who ran a black health clinic in the Eastern Cape; Dimza Pityana of the South African Institute of Race Relations; and other professional women prominent in their communities — social workers, nurses, teachers, churchwomen, journalists. Some, like Mamphela Ramphele and a journalist, Thenjiwe Mtintso, were banned on their release from detention.

Many young people were detained, and many of them tortured. Too numerous to list here, their experience is illustrated by that of Mpho Theoabale. She was a 16-year-old Soweto student who lived through the events of June 1976, including the original decision to boycott classes and the planning of the march on 16 June, when she saw many of her friends killed or wounded. The police violence prompted the students to further demonstrations against buildings and beerhalls owned by the government; they appealed to their parents to stay away from work and join in their demonstrations. Mpho was arrested herself, held incommunicado for six weeks, during which she was beaten in attempts to make her 'confess' to sabotage or turn state witness against her friends, and finally released, when she fled the country. She is one of a large number of young people who have left South Africa to carry on the struggle outside. Another was Thandi Modise, mentioned earlier, who returned as an ANC combatant and is now in prison.

The Black Women's Federation was one of those organisations which had emerged in the wake of the repression of the 1960s when organisations opposed to apartheid had been either destroyed or driven underground. When it had still been possible for organisations to operate legally, the influence of women in national liberation organisations had begun to grow, and their participation at all levels had become more and more important. The Women's League of the ANC was no longer simply fulfilling the role of background support for the activities more usually organised by men; and individual women were achieving positions of importance and influence. Impetus to the growing strength and importance of the women's role was given by the FSAW. But with the period of intense repression that followed the Sharpeville massacre of 1960, the Federation found its leading members all banned or placed under house arrest. The ANC was outlawed, and this meant that the ANC Women's League was also illegal, cutting away mass organised support for the Federation, even though it was not declared illegal. For years leading women lived under precarious conditions, frequently detained, always restricted — most of them were, by law, not even permitted to speak to each other.

With the end in 1961 of the long era of non-violent activities, women, and their former organisations, became part of the underground resistance and the general preparations for armed struggle to end apartheid. Other women turned towards activities to ease their day-to-day burdens, organising self-help associations and establishing day-care centres for children, and feeding programmes.

In the 1970s a new generation of young people, women and men, began to organise around what became known as the black consciousness movement. In December 1975, 210 delegates representing 41 organisations gathered in Durban to found the Black Women's Federation (BWF). Its purpose was outlined by its first president, Dr Fatima Meer. It was mainly 'to galvanize black women, to bring them together and consolidate grievances and create opportunities for them to do something to help themselves and to help the general South African situation move towards change'.[26] The BWF worked in both urban and rural areas. They compiled a booklet for African women to inform them of their legal rights. They started literacy, nutrition and health classes, and tried to establish small cottage industries. They worked on practical issues, launching a scheme to slash the expense of compulsory school uniforms for black pupils by buying material wholesale, making it up and selling direct to the parents.

Within a year, seven leading BWF women were detained. Fatima Meer was banned. And in October 1977, the entire organisation was banned. Other black consciousness organisations suffered a similar fate.[27]

Raids were followed by prolonged detention, and finally charges against some. Several women activists were banned.

Re-organising

The vacuum left by the banning of the BWF was soon filled, as new organisations formed or old ones re-emerged.

During recent years a number of women's organisations have been struggling to the forefront in various parts of the country. As yet there is no national organisation of the scope of the Women's Federation, and the formation of a nation-wide organisation under today's especially repressive conditions would be a formidable task. The systematic banning, exiling or jailing of women who emerge in political struggle is only one of the many handicaps.

The United Women's Organisation (UWO) was established in the Cape in April 1981 at a conference attended by more than 300 women from 31 different localities in the Western Cape. Many were women who had past experience of political, trade union or community organisation. 'We cannot abstract ourselves from political issues because they are our daily life . . . Our place must be as part of the struggle for fundamental rights.' Both the policy and constitution of the UWO stress the need for women to fight for 'the removal of all laws, conventions, regulations, customs, that discriminate against women'. The need for democracy and the need for the liberation of women are the foundation of the UWO.[28] Two thousand people organised by UWO celebrated 9 August, Women's Day, in 1981.

People could see that we were doing good, but we were still weak. But the things that were happening here now have really opened the people's eyes. We women were locked up because we cannot afford the rent increases. We suffered together.

In the police vans we told the women about UWO and why they should join. They can see that it is important to come and fight our problems together.

So now more and more women are joining UWO. We have had enough of suffering. We have had enough of poor conditions. We have decided to fight all our problems together with one voice.

(Lucy Ninzi, a member of the United Women's Organisations, active in the Western Cape — Grassroots, October 1983)

The FSAW has re-emerged, and continues as far as possible in the tradition of the original Federation. Calling itself FEDSAW, it was one of the initiators of the Free Mandela Campaign launched in 1981 to call for the release of Nelson Mandela and all political prisoners, and has been involved in campaigns to save the lives of ANC members sentenced to death, and has mobilised support for their families, as well as for political prisoners, detainees and banned people and their families. It was one of the initiators of a call in 1981 to set up regional committees to co-ordinate a campaign to boycott the celebration of the twentieth anniversary of the founding in 1961 of the white republic. It has also taken up 'grassroots' issues, fighting against rent and bus fare increases, against forced removals, and for health and childcare facilities. When school pupils have been engaged in protests and boycotts, it has expressed its solidarity with them. In 1981, on the twenty-fifth anniversary of the 1956 demonstration against the pass laws, it held a very successful celebration.

The UWO and FEDSAW, the one based in the Western Cape and the other mainly in the Transvaal, are the most prominent of the organisations mobilising women on the basis of resistance to apartheid. There are others, such as the Natal Organisation of Women, formed in 1983 with similar aims and objectives. The organisation Black Women Unite was founded in 1981 in the tradition of the earlier black consciousness organisations; based in Soweto, it was said in 1984 to have committees in a number of towns.[29]

The best-known and most active organisation among white women is the Black Sash. It was established in 1955 with the limited objective at that time of protesting against the removal of Coloured voters from the common roll. From the first, the women's actions took the form of silent vigils, and the protestors were recognised by the black sashes which they wore draped across from shoulder to waist, a sign of mourning for the Constitution.

From this their vigils extended to protests against other apartheid laws, particularly those that had the harshest effects on family life. Today the Black Sash has opened its ranks to women of all groups and has concentrated its work on the evils arising from mass removals, migrant labour and the destruction of family life. It conducts Advice Offices for those caught in the net of apartheid laws, and publishes a magazine. The Black Sash is not a political campaigning organisation, and does not set out to organise women as a whole. But its work has resulted in keeping some of the most potent issues affecting women before the white public, and the reports resulting from its investigations are of great value. Some of the despair felt by women who have battled for years against heart-breaking injustice is reflected in the words of a leading member in October 1980:

> We have failed abysmally, not through want of trying. Peaceful protest and reasoned arguments have failed and young people today have lost their patience and resorted to what seems to be mindless violence. [They] are tired of waiting to be given their rights peacefully . . . However, believing that 'for evil to succeed it is sufficient for good men to do nothing', we will . . . go on bashing our heads against a stone wall hoping for a miracle.[30]

Yet the Black Sash continues with research, advice and propaganda and with its silent protests, as the voice of those white women who, while living in well-endowed conditions, cannot accept the cruelty inflicted by apartheid on their black sisters.

There has never been a parallel organisation among white men, although the issues on which the Black Sash campaigns are of equal interest to men. This may reflect the fact that the men of the white middle class have a much closer involvement in the economic structure of apartheid than do the women.

A number of women's organisations grew out of white women's concern at the Soweto uprisings of 1976. Women for Peace, convened by Mrs Harry Oppenheimer, wife of the diamond and gold millionaire, heard at its inaugural meeting first-hand accounts of Soweto massacres, such as that from Mrs Sally Khali of a Soweto nursery creche, whose tiny charges saw police shoot down eight children on the open space near their creche. The women hoped to bring about change through peaceful co-operation and understanding. But there is a chasm between women who pray for peace and those whose very lives are a form of war. 'Contact with white women has given black women very little reason to feel a shared sense of oppression', stated Ms Janet Shapiro, a lecturer at Rhodes University. 'There does certainly seem to be not much basis for sisterhood, and unless and until such time as black and white women share the same economic reality I cannot see much hope for any movement in South Africa that takes universal sisterhood as its starting point.'[31]

Mobilising today

The revival in the early 1980s of the FSAW, and the development of other women's organisations opposed to apartheid have been a major factor in advancing the unity and active involvement of women on all fronts.

In every region organisations have emerged which stand for a non-racial undivided South Africa and which share the view that women's organisations have a key political role in the total struggle for liberation.

Their response is shown by the fact that women's organisations opposed to apartheid reflect the broad trends in the general mobilisation of resistance during this period, by mostly being oriented towards, or affiliated to, the United Democratic Front. Amongst the exceptions is Black Women Unite, which has linked itself to a smaller national grouping of organisations, the National Forum.

In other ways too the mobilisation of women has paralleled the mobilisation of general popular resistance. In 1981 the organisations, in particular FEDSAW and UWO, took up issues as they came up, supporting campaigns or protests of a temporary and limited nature. These included protests at rent increases, boycotts in support of strikes and the campaign against the celebrations of the twentieth anniversary of the founding of the apartheid republic. But soon both organisations were explicitly seeking forms of more permanent mobilisation and organisation of women. They set themselves a double objective. Recognising the social barriers to the organisation and political activities of black women under apartheid (described in this book), they gave their attention to promoting the organisation of women into smaller localised groups dealing with immediate issues. This included encouraging women to join and work in trade unions. In this way the women in smaller organisations, concentrating on local and grassroots issues, could also be drawn into the national political campaigns.[32]

The effects of this were evident by 1984, a year of general mass mobilisation of popular resistance. In the early part of the year, for example, FEDSAW was active in promoting the establishment of local organisations of women in black residential areas throughout the

108

Transvaal, from the industrial areas of the Pretoria-Witwatersrand-Vereeniging Triangle, to rural and semi-rural areas in the Northern Transvaal. Depending on the area and the needs of women, the organisations brought women together on issues ranging from increases in rents and other aspects of the cost of living, or educational demands, to the setting up in rural areas of co-operatives for the production, distribution or purchase of daily needs. In Coloured and Indian residential areas organisation centred around opposition to the regime's constitutional proposals and the elections in August 1984 to the Coloured and Indian chambers of the segregated parliament. In areas with anti-apartheid civic associations, the new local women's organisations were often linked to them. They were also generally affiliated directly or indirectly to the UDF, which was engaged in mobilising people in opposition to the new parliament and to the regime's local government structures for administering African residential areas outside the bantustans.[33]

Taking a similar path, the UWO issued a call in 1983 for women to bring the organisations they were part of into the UDF.[34]

Thus the mobilisation of women into local activities with immediate and limited demands has become woven into the total resistance to apartheid.

In line with these developments, the meetings in 1984 to mark South African Women's Day (9 August) took place in more areas than previously. They attracted more people and involved more campaigning activity. These meetings, held in the weeks preceding the parliamentary elections, highlighted opposition to the new parliamentary constitution and related issues. In the Transvaal women's groups came together after local celebrations for a mass rally under the theme 'Women unite against Botha's new deal'.[35] At a meeting in Cape Town where the focus of activities was on support for squatters threatened with removal from the Western Cape, a speaker said: 'People are being attacked once again by the government. Today we do not just celebrate the women's action in the past: we ask how women will fight against the new constitution.'[36]

While the participation of women in the open, legal sphere of the liberation struggle has become increasingly visible in recent years, the role of women in the underground struggle is more difficult to discern. It can be glimpsed only fragmentarily through the repressive actions of the regime and its agents, directed both at those working in underground structures and against those in exile.

Since the mid-1970s, as noted in an earlier section, women have appeared in trials — and in some cases been imprisoned — on charges ranging from possessing banned literature, recruiting people to join the ANC, recruiting people for military training, or undergoing military training and participating in armed action. At the time of writing one woman was being held in detention in connection with the find of an arms cache in the Eastern Transvaal, while another was facing trial in the Northern Transvaal on charges which included recruiting for the ANC, and a third had been convicted in Johannesburg of furthering the aims of the ANC.

The regime and its agents pursue those who oppose it even in exile. The deaths of Jabu Nzima, of Ruth First, of Jeannette Schoon and her six-year-old daughter Katryn, show the price that women may pay for unyielding opposition to apartheid. These three women and Katryn were all blown to pieces by bombs while living in exile.

Jabu Nzima was living in exile in Swaziland. She and her husband, former organisers of SACTU and ANC activists, were killed in 1982 by a bomb planted in their car. Ruth First, writer, academic, teacher and organiser, was killed in 1982 by a letter bomb in Maputo, Mozambique, where she headed a research team at the Centre for African Studies. Jeannette and her daughter were killed in 1983 by a parcel bomb in Lubango, Angola, where she and her husband had gone as volunteers to teach English at the university.

Voice of women

In spite of the intense repression the voice of women who have always been deeply immersed in the struggle of their own people still emerges. Young and angry, old and undefeated, their continuing defiance in the face of prosecution, torture, and terrible loss, challenges apartheid, destroys myths of female submissiveness and subservience.

'I stand unafraid! I stand defiant! I stand sorry for the government, its supporters and puppets . . .!' declared Florence Mkhize, formerly active in the ANC Women's League, and an organiser in the first FSAW, as soon as her ban expired in 1980 and she was able to appear in public.[37]

Eighty-two-year-old Dora Tamana (who died in 1983), a founder of the Women's Federation, spoke at the inaugural conference of the United Women's Organisation (UWO) in 1981, calling on the women to organise.

> You who have no work — speak! You who have no homes — speak! You who have no schools — speak! You who have to run like chickens from the vulture — speak! We must free ourselves! Men and women must share housework. Men and women must work together in the home and in the world . . . I opened the door for you — you must go forward!

Annie Silinga, who died in 1984 aged 74, defiantly refused all her life to carry a pass, despite the harassment and hardship that this brought, including the fact that without a pass she could not claim a pension, although she was both old and disabled. A life-long activist in the ANC and Women's League before they were banned, an accused in the 1956 Treason Trial, and a patron of the newly-formed United Democratic Front, she was addressing meetings up to two days before she died. 'I will never carry a pass', she said, 'All people of this country should have the right to move freely.'

Seventy-two-year-old Mrs Greta Ncapai stated in the Rand Supreme Court that she had been arrested so many times in her life she had lost count. 'I was in and out of John Vorster Square, Marshall Square, Protea Police Station so many times, it has been too often to count. When I was arrested again last year it was just one of those things.' Cross-examined on her attitude to the ANC and violence, Mrs Ncapai said, 'I will support anything that will bring change in this country.'

While the struggle for justice and freedom in South Africa is constantly renewed by courageous young people who, unarmed, face the guns and tanks of the regime, it is also astonishing how older women maintain their activities in the face of years and years of bannings, imprisonment and other forms of action against themselves or their families.

Where young ANC militants have been sent by the apartheid regime to the gallows, personal loss and grief do not deter the women from voicing their hatred of apartheid.

After her son, Solomon Mahlangu, became the first guerilla fighter to be executed, Martha Mahlangu appeared at a public meeting in Soweto. Defiantly draped in the green, black and gold colours of the illegal ANC, she declared it was disgraceful for black mothers to stand and watch their children dying for their motherland without joining the struggle. 'Nothing is going to stop blacks from being free', she said.

The words of Sarah Mosololi, mother of Jerry, on the morning her son was executed in 1983 together with two other young ANC fighters, resound like a poem: 'Go well my son, I love you. I am proud of you because you are to die for your people. We'll meet where you're going. You must know the struggle will not end even after your death.'

The mother of Naphtali Manana (saved from the gallows, with two others condemned to death, after a world-wide campaign) asserted her militant faith in the future despite her son's lifelong prison sentence: 'I see a future holding victory for us. Our great-grandfathers fought with their hands and they were defeated. Our children fight with guns, and they will win.'[38]

Faith in the inevitable destruction of apartheid has given Albertina Nontsikelelo Sisulu strength and courage during 40 years of political struggle and persecution. She joined the ANC Women's League at the time of its formation, and later was a leading figure in the Women's Federation. She was banned for longer than anyone else — 18 years —

during which time she brought up her own five children, together with the two children of her deceased sister, while her husband, Walter Sisulu, has spent more than 20 years on Robben Island — sentenced to life imprisonment together with Nelson Mandela. She and her eldest son, Max, were arrested and detained in 1964 (Max was then only 16) during the trial of her husband. Her daughter, Lindiwe, is in exile after being detained for 11 months, assaulted and tortured. Her son Zwelakhe was detained for a year. Yet as soon as her bans had expired Albertina was once more in the thick of the fight against apartheid. She was elected one of the three Presidents of the United Democratic Front, and has endured subsequent arrests.

Winnie Mandela exemplifies the creative capacities of women under the most adverse circumstances. When she was finally banished from her home after years of harassment, detention, imprisonment and constant arrests, she was sent to live in a tiny matchbox of a house, without running water, a bathroom or electric light, in an area for Africans behind a small hill, out of sight of the white inhabitants of the country town of Brandfort. The place where she lived had no name. It was called 'the black location'. There she was forced — and this was still the case at the time of writing — to exist under severe banning orders that prohibited her from speaking to more than one person at a time, or from receiving visitors in her own home. Yet there she organised a mobile clinic to tour the district and a babycare centre, and taught the miserably paid workers how to grow their own vegetables and how to demand higher wages.

A New Zealand journalist interviewed Winnie Mandela in 1982 in this remote place. She spoke of how resistance to racialist laws had helped build the stature of the black woman. She spoke of the retrogressive aspects of the culture of her people, and how women had both to fight the racist regime and to fight against traditional customs. 'I, as a black woman, am an eternal minor.' But these issues had conscientised the black woman, and she has emerged fighting all the way — 'one of the greatest resisters and, I believe, when we shall bring about the liberation of this land, the women will be in the forefront, emerging not only as martyrs . . . [but] as one of the greatest weapons, the greatest instruments, of liberation'.

Dr Ramphele, taken from her home in King Williamstown and dumped in an isolated place in Lenyenye over seven hundred miles away, in six years of this banishment built a clinic to serve 50,000 poor people scattered around the area; and among other achievements established a literacy programme, a brick co-operative run by women, a library, a bursary fund, and in-the-field lectures on sanitation and dental care.[39]

Persecution does not necessarily cease with release from detention or the completion of a jail sentence. Fatima Meer's home was attacked by gunmen; another woman, Sheila Weinberg had to have a seven-foot wall built round her house as protection against continued attacks.

Lilian Ngoyi, former President of the Women's Federation, lived the last 18 years of her life (she died in 1982) banned and silenced, struggling to earn money by sewing in her tiny house. Yet in one of the brief periods when one set of bans had expired and the new ones had not yet been imposed, she told a journalist of the hardships, then rose to her feet and said, 'You can tell my friends all over the world that this girl is still her old self . . . I am looking forward to the day when my children will share in the wealth of our lovely South Africa.' 'For her', wrote a journalist on her death, 'the freedom struggle was like a call'.

V. Looking Forward

The many years of white-minority rule have seen the systematic and continued denial of black aspirations in all fields, stemming in the first place from total black exclusion from all positions of effective state power. The maintenance of such exclusion has necessitated the introduction of ever more repressive legislation and actions, together with enormous growth in military spending and political influence of the armed forces. The much-vaunted constitutional changes introduced in 1984, and which incorporate a small section of the Indian and Coloured communities into a segregated, undemocratic parliament under white control still leave the majority excluded from central government.

The economic changes of recent years have been profound, altering the basis of labour needs, and by the elimination of large sections of unskilled labour rendering whole sections of the population superfluous. The vast scale of modern agriculture needs machines and a smaller amount of semi-skilled or skilled labour, supplemented by seasonal unskilled labour; this latter work is today usually performed by women. Industry is undergoing the same process. It is not unique to South Africa but the method of dealing with the 'surplus' labour by means of the bantustan and migrant labour systems is unique, and its impact on women particularly harsh.

These changes have been accompanied on the economic front by industrial and commercial development that has brought great prosperity to white South Africa even during periods of economic recession, now enjoying one of the highest standards of living in the world: measured in purely material terms, white women in particular have attained a life of exceptional privilege.

For the vast majority of African women, their lives have undergone substantial change, but they have not progressed towards a better life. On the contrary, their position is worse than it has ever been. Always the greatest victims of the system, they have become greater victims in a system whose anomalies increase.

Many claims have been made by the apartheid regime concerning the 'changing face' of apartheid. Fringe benefits have filtered down to a small section of blacks, so the casual visitor, seeing African men and women in the large towns in a variety of visible jobs that were closed to them a few years ago (cashiers in supermarkets, shop assistants and bank clerks) and noticing the relaxation of strict apartheid rules in some hotels and restaurants, or more Africans driving their own cars, receive the impression of change. But for all the acquisition of privileges the small African 'middle class' remains outside the laager of white society and white power; they are still segregated; they still carry passes or documents showing exemptions. They are still denied access to social, economic and political power. The few, as with bantustan leaders, who are taken into the system become as despotic as their white masters. They do not represent the majority, who do not benefit by their private accumulation of showy houses and cars.

In many ways the lives of women have altered more substantially over the past few years than those of men. Women are becoming the heads of families to an ever-increasing extent, depending less than ever in the past on men for their survival and for the creation of a reasonable life, their independence and self-assurance is altering relationships.

The most oppressed and deprived women are the five million now living in the bantustans, trapped by the merciless constraints of apartheid that permit them no freedom of movement to seek work, to try and climb out of the pit of abysmal poverty and deprivation into which they have been cast. Mostly perpetual minors in law, denied rights over property and children, they are always subject to the authority of men. Yet even here, within this system, there is an increasing number of rural households headed by women. As Jacklyn Cock states, this contradiction between their subordinate existence and independent status further sharpens the edge of their disabilities.[1]

Yet women, contending with the devastating material conditions in the bantustans described in earlier pages, oppressed and deprived in every aspect of their lives, have emerged with militancy and confidence, with persistency and strength, in the struggle.

There seem to be vast contradictions between their status and deprivation, and on the other hand their strength and positive defiance.

The contradictions have entered the home. Many men in the liberation movements have shown an ambivalent attitude towards the women's movement, recognising the necessity for the organisation of women and for their part in political struggles, but sometimes resenting both the personal inconveniences (as in the two episodes in 1913 ad 1958, when many husbands paid fines to release their wives from jail) and also the threat of the abrogation of their own power over women. Yet women have often changed men's attitudes through their activities, as in the 1956 demonstration to Pretoria, which many men viewed with surprise and with awe, and which produced from men, who cared for children while the women were demonstrating, a co-operation that had not been evident in the past.

115

During the past few years there has been increasing recognition within the male-dominated organisations of the need for men to change their own attitudes; that the struggle itself demands the full and equal participation of the women. Speaking at the first conference of the Women's Section of the ANC held outside South Africa, in 1981, the President, Oliver Tambo, stated:

> If we are to engage our full potential in pursuit of the goals of our revolutionary struggle, then, as revolutionaries, we should stop pretending that women in our movement have the same opportunities as men . . . On the other hand, women should stop behaving as if there was no place for them above the level of certain categories of involvement. They have a duty to liberate us men from antique concepts and attitudes about the place and role of women in society . . . The oppressor has, at best, a lesser duty to liberate the oppressed than the oppressed themselves. The struggle to conquer oppression in our country is the weaker for the traditionalist, conservative and primitive restraints imposed on women by man-dominated structures within our movement, as also because of equally traditionalist attitudes of surrender and submission on the part of women.[2]

Much more explicit attention is now being paid to the question of the emancipation of women and the role of women in the liberation struggles than ever in the past.

South African women are not indifferent to the feminist movements of other countries, and the literature of feminism has given impetus to research into the history and activities of women, and into the lives of women today, in areas that have never before been investigated. These are not mere academic exercises: they reveal circumstances, beliefs and changing attitudes that make it possible to open the way for a greater participation of women in the struggle for freedom, as well as uncovering the past history of women's struggles.

But at the same time women of developed countries can draw much from the struggle of women in South Africa. The fight to change their status is a political one because, without the ending of apartheid, there can never be any liberation for women. That is why the struggle to liberate women is also a part of the total struggle for liberation. Participating in it sharpens the women's perceptions of patriarchal oppression, whether rooted in colonial or in precolonial origins. Women must contend with this, nor can it be forgotten, for it holds them back from full participation in the fight to liberate South Africa.

116

Many Western feminists see the family as the seat of male primacy and of patriarchal oppression, maintaining that it has been the domestication of women, turning them into unpaid producers and reproducers, that has codified their oppression. But to women of South Africa the right to family life, to live as a family unit, remains a primary demand, and one that strikes at the very structure of apartheid — the migrant labour system.

All the issues that concern feminists in other countries must be seen in this context: sexual oppression, male chauvinism, discrimination within the law relating to employment, the need for divorce reform, reform of abortion laws — it is not that South African women are not concerned with these issues. It is that for a considerable proportion of the female population, these issues cannot arise in such specific ways.

> Before one can speak of equal pay for equal work, one has to speak of the provision of work; before one can speak of re-forming divorce law, one has to speak of abolishing the basis of the law which has created this distorted and perverted form of capitalist family ... It is only the abolition of this and all its refinements that can alter their situation in any material sense.[3]

In South Africa black women, the most vulnerable of all people within the apartheid state, have been forced to embark on a struggle that takes them beyond their own specific oppression. The struggle of South African women for recognition as equal citizens with equal opportunities is primarily the struggle against apartheid, for national liberation. Nor is it a question of putting one first, then taking up the other. The victory of this struggle against apartheid is the absolute condition for any fundamental change in the social status of women; the participation of the women in this struggle is the absolute condition for its success. The participation of the women is an expression not only of their desire to rid all South Africa of the curse of apartheid, but also of their deep concern for their own status as women.

Thus under the conditions of apartheid South Africa's oppressed women cannot limit their objectives to those of simply trying to establish their legal rights in a modern industrialised society, nor can they hope to emerge with a few privileges in a male-dominated world. Instead they participate in the movement to destroy the whole basis of racial exploitation, and to open up the prospect of free development for both women and men. This is based on the understanding that the liberation of women is not simply a matter of amending laws or changing male attitudes, but of the fundamental restructuring of a society towards the aims of freedom and justice for all.

The struggle against apartheid has entered its most difficult and hardest phase: a time of confrontation when political struggle takes many different forms, of legality and illegality, of organisation and protest within the limitations of the suppressive regime, and of underground organisation and violent conflict.

The women of South Africa, always an integral part of this struggle, remain a key to its strength and mass development. They have come a long way: they have a long way to go.

Tables

The sources of information used in the tables are given in the relevant parts of the References (indicated below in the case of each table).

TABLE I: Population of South Africa: 1983

The total population of South Africa in 1983 was estimated as just over 31 million divided by apartheid into separate groups:

African:	22.7 million	73.1%
Coloured:	2.8 million	8.9%
Asian:	0.9 million	2.8%
White:	4.5 million	15.3%

Source: Official census figures and other estimates *(see Note 1, Introduction).*

TABLE II: Workforce-migrants and commuters: 1980

According to the official statistics, of the estimated total African workforce of 5.4 million in 1980, one quarter (24.1 per cent) were migrant or contract workers. Another 13 per cent were 'commuters' making a total of nearly 40 per cent who were officially regarded as being resident outside the part of South Africa in which they worked more or less permanently. Just under half the African workforce (46 per cent) was both working and recognised as permanently resident outside the bantustans.[1]

Source: Official 1980 Census figures *(see Note 1, Part I).*

TABLE III: Marital status: 1980

		Total	Married	Unmarried
African:	Number	8,227,680	1,917,280	5,491,680
	Per cent	100.0	23.3	76.7
White:	Number	2,262,700	1,033,640	954,420
	Per cent	100.0	46.0	54.0

Source: Official 1980 Census figures *(see Note 10, Part I).*

TABLE IV: Women arrested under the Pass Laws: 1979-1983

These figures do not give the total numbers arrested, as those given for arrests by Administration board officials are only for the main urban areas of South Africa.

	Women arrested by SA Police: whole country	Women arrested by Administration Boards: main urban areas only	Total arrests of women and men under pass laws: whole country
1979	20,209	13,823	203,266
1980	14,653	16,794	158,355
1981	14,038	21,508	162,022
1982	16,532	27,991	206,022
1983	27,096	17,651	262,904

Source: Official figures given in response to questions in parliament, 1980-84 *(see Note 19, Part I).*

TABLE V: Infant mortality rates in various urban centres: 1970-1980

City	Year	White	Coloured	Indian	African
		Deaths per 1,000 live births			
Port Elizabeth	1970	—	—	—	330.00
Johannesburg	1970	20.00	—	—	95.00
Grahamstown	1970	—	—	—	188.00
Bloemfontein	1972	—	—	—	170.00
East London	1972	—	—	—	107.00
Cape Town	1973	—	—	—	63.00
Cape Town	1981	9.40	18.80	20.40	34.60
Pretoria	1980	10.08	53.48	11.98	53.13

Source: Government health reports: *(see Note 74, Part II).*

TABLE VI: Increase of women in the black workforce by sector: 1973-1981

Sector/Industry	Per cent increase
Shoe	23.9
Commerce	15.2
Electrical machinery	15.0
Textile	12.1
Clothing	7.2
Non-metal mineral	3.6
Food	3.5
Furniture	2.9
Chemical	2.0
Wood	2.9

Source: National Manpower Surveys, 1973-81 *(see Note 61, Part IV).*

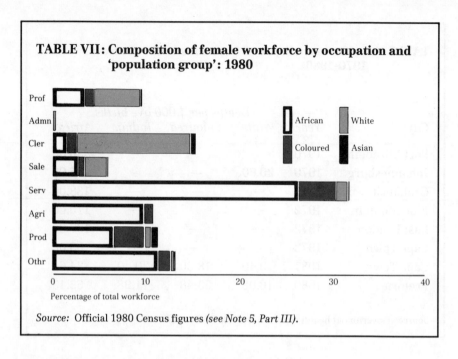

TABLE VII: Composition of female workforce by occupation and 'population group': 1980

Source: Official 1980 Census figures *(see Note 5, Part III).*

Key to abbreviations used in graphs:

Tables VII, VIII

Prof	Professional
Admn	Administrative
Cler	Clerical
Sale	Sales
Serv	Services (incl. domestic service)
Agri	Agriculture
Prod	Production
Othr	Other

Table IX

Elec	Electricity
Mine	Mining
Cons	Construction
Tran	Transport
Agri	Agriculture
Manu	Manufacturing
Comm	Commerce
Serv	Services (incl. domestic service)
Unem	Unemployed

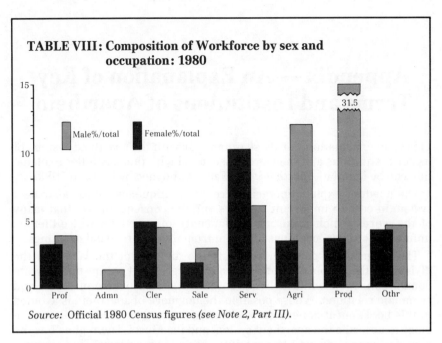

TABLE VIII: Composition of Workforce by sex and occupation: 1980

Male%/total   Female%/total

31.5

| | Prof | Admn | Cler | Sale | Serv | Agri | Prod | Othr |

Source: Official 1980 Census figures *(see Note 2, Part III).*

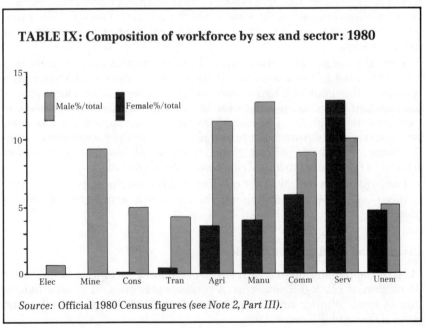

TABLE IX: Composition of workforce by sex and sector: 1980

Male%/total   Female%/total

| | Elec | Mine | Cons | Tran | Agri | Manu | Comm | Serv | Unem |

Source: Official 1980 Census figures *(see Note 2, Part III).*

Appendix — An Explanation of Key Terms and Institutions of Apartheid

This is an explanation, for those unfamiliar with the apartheid system, of its key institutions and the words associated with them. A fuller explanation can be found in *Apartheid: The Facts,* published by IDAF in 1983.

The need for explanation arises from the uniqueness of the apartheid system in certain important respects and the consequent fact that many of the words which make up the language of apartheid will either be unfamiliar or have meanings different from their more usual meanings.

The language of apartheid reflects the division of the land and the division of the people of South Africa into segregated groups under white domination, even while it helps obscure the real nature of social and economic relations. Where possible the language of apartheid is avoided in this book, but it is necessary to make some use of the official terminology to describe the apartheid system and its effects. The regime has the power to create and maintain institutions and impose laws. Those institutions and laws are part of the reality which does in fact divide the population into separate groups whose lives are regulated and constrained in different ways.

Naturally the power of the regime to impose its own terms and its own ideas is limited in the same ways as its power to prevent resistance, as a reading of this book will make clear. This limitation is also manifested in the constant alteration of words for key relationships and practices. For example, the majority of the black section of the population has been successively called *Native, Bantu* and now *Black* by the government, while the name for the basic policies of the system has shifted from *apartheid* to *separate development* to *plural relations* to *co-operation*.

The explanation below is set out under three headings, corresponding to three basic aspects of apartheid. The terms of apartheid are printed in bold type.

Dividing the Land and the People

Most of the population of South Africa, estimated in 1983 to be just over 31 million, is black (85 per cent). A fundamental division of apartheid is that of land. Whites, only 15 per cent of the population, are allocated most of the land (87 per cent).

The words used to label people take on special meanings under apartheid. The principal terms are **Asian, Black, Coloured** and **White.**

The black majority is split by apartheid into three main **population groups.** The largest of these groups is today officially, and confusingly, labelled **Black** and comprises most of those more usually referred to as African (signifying their descent from those who inhabited the area before the colonial period). Previous terms used for this group by the rulers of South Africa were **Native** and **Bantu.** The term **Coloured** is used to refer to several groups of people including descendants of those who originally lived in the areas in the Cape where Europeans first settled and most people whose descent is traced from members of more than one 'population group', as well as descendants of Malay slaves brought in the early days of the Cape Colony. The small group called **Asian** consists mainly of descendants of workers brought from India during the nineteenth century.

The people in all these groups reject apartheid labels, choosing rather to call themselves all 'black'.

The section of the population classified **White** is treated as a single privileged group even though its members speak different languages and have different cultural and historical backgrounds.

A basic aspect of apartheid is the exclusion of the African majority of the population from participation in central government. They are expected instead to meet their political aspirations in subordinate political structures based on the smaller part of the country to which they are assigned. This consists of numerous scattered, poverty-stricken and fragmented areas. Previously called **Reserves** they are now grouped into ten units officially called **Homelands,** reflecting the attempt of the government to suggest that they are the homes of those assigned to them. They are presented as the territories of separate **National States.** In this book as is common amongst opponents of apartheid, they are referred to as bantustans. Every African is assigned to a bantustan, irrespective of whether they were born there or have ever lived there. When the regime declares a bantustan **Independent,** all those who have been allocated to it lose their South African nationality.

The regime tries to present its policies regarding the bantustans as aimed at promoting the development of those areas, and used the term **Separate Development** to describe it. In reality apartheid has promoted underdevelopment and poverty has grown.

Outside the bantustans, Africans are required to live in restricted residential areas called **Townships** (formerly **Locations**), or in the case of many migrant workers *(see below)* in **Hostels** or **Compounds** at mines or large industrial concerns. The **Group Areas Policy** is used to divide towns and cities into segregated zones **(Group Areas)** set aside for

125

residence, commercial activities and industry for members of the **White, Coloured** and **Asian** groups (each in separate zones). Based on these group areas are segregated local government structures, and a segregated tricameral parliament with separate White, Coloured and Indian chambers, designed to preserve white political power while extending limited participation in central government to small sections of the Indian and Coloured communities.

The majority of the population in South Africa is united in rejecting the segregated political structures of apartheid.

Forced Removal of Population

The apartheid regime has sought to enforce strict territorial segregation of the different 'population groups'. People are forcibly evicted from their homes if they are in a zone which the government has asigned to another group. The government speaks, not of forced removal or eviction, but of **Relocation** and **Resettlement.** The evictions take place in many different kinds of areas and under different laws.

In rural areas people are moved on a number of different pretexts. The places in which they live may be designated **Black Spots** — these are areas of land occupied and owned by Africans which the government has designated for another group, usually white. The occupiers are moved to a bantustan. Others are moved in the course of **Consolidation** of the bantustans, as the regime attempts to reduce the number of fragments of land which make up the bantustans. Over a million black tenants have been evicted from white owned farms since the 1960s. Tenants who paid cash rent to the farms were called **Squatters,** implying they had no right to be on the land. In the process of removal most of those affected lose access to land for cultivation, and most are put into **Resettlement Camps,** some of which are called **Closer Settlements** (urban-type settlements in remote rural areas, most of whose residents have no access to agricultural land).

The term **Squatters** is also applied to people who occupy land for residence in or near urban areas without official permission. Because of the shortage of housing created by policies designed to back up influx control *(see below)*, vast squatter communities have grown up in major urban areas.

Where the communities lie outside bantustans, the government constantly tries to evict the residents and destroy their accommodation.

Another process of removal in urban areas has taken the form of the concentration of black people into larger and more sharply segregated regional townships, usually situated further away from city centres. As applied to the Indian and Coloured communities this has involved the

126

Group Areas Act. If a bantustan is situated close enough, Africans have been moved into new townships within their boundaries, to become **Commuters,** travelling each day or week to work in the 'white' areas. This process has also involved an attempt to locate industries close to or inside bantustans, the so-called **Border Industry** policy, which is now part of a policy described as **Decentralisation.**

Control of Movement

For the majority of people in South Africa there is no freedom of movement in their own country. Their movement is controlled by a system of regulations known as **Pass Laws,** which apply only to Africans, and which form part of the policy and practice of **Influx control.** Every African over 16 years of age must carry a set of identity documents known as a **Pass.** The government now calls the pass a **Reference Book** or, in the case of people from the so called 'independent' bantustans, a **Passport.** They may be renamed yet again and called **Identity Documents.**

The country outside the bantustans is divided for the purpose of influx control into **Prescribed Areas** (which include all cities and most industrial and commercial areas, where most employment opportunities exist) and **Non-prescribed Areas** (largely farm land and mines). The right of Africans to remain in such areas is linked to employment and housing. The implementation of the pass laws outside the bantustans is carried out largely by what were until recently called **Administration Boards** and are now called **Development Boards.** They work closely with the police and labour bureaux *(see below).*

Africans may live on white-owned farmland if permitted to do so by the farmer who employs them. If ordered off the land they must go to a bantustan and can only move to the towns through the **Migrant labour** system operated through the **Labour Bureaux.** All African men of working age (15-65 years old) must register with the labour bureau in their area, unless they are self-employed. All women who are seeking employment must register. On registration a worker is classified for a particular category of work. No one may leave an area to seek work without permission from the bureau. To obtain employment a worker must be requisitioned through the labour bureau system and become a **Contract Worker:** a contract of employment is attested by the labour bureau. Contracts are normally for a maximum of a year, and must be renewed at the same labour bureau. A worker cannot be employed in any other category of work other than that for which he or she has been registered, without the agreement of the labour office.

127

Those who avoid the system and go to the towns or cities to find work on their own are described as **Illegals.**

The presence and movement of Africans in the prescribed areas are regulated by various pass laws. Those whose passes are not in order may be **Endorsed Out,** that is to say, an endorsement is put in their pass book and they are sent to a bantustan or a farming area. Many others are fined or imprisoned. The conditions under which Africans may remain in prescribed areas are set out in **Section 10** of the (Blacks) Urban Areas Act. It stipulates that no one may remain in an urban area longer than 72 hours unless he or she: (a) has lived there continuously in the area since birth or (b) has worked continuously for a single employer for 10 years or for different employers for 15 years; or (c) is the wife or dependent child of someone who has rights (a) or (b); or (d) has permission from the manager of the local labour bureau to be there for more than 72 hours. This last category consists mainly of migrant, or contract labourers.

The government has repeatedly said that the pass laws would be scrapped. Some of the changes which have occurred are only in the words used (the legislation used to extend passes to women in the 1950s was called the 'Abolition of Passes and Co-ordination of Documents Act', because the passes were renamed as 'reference books'). Real changes which have occurred have benefited only a small minority. As far as the majority are concerned, the system of pass laws, influx control and labour bureaux has become steadily more effective in restricting their movement and in maintaining a supply of cheap labour for the white-owned economy.

Inside a government shelter at 'Compensation Farm' resettlement camp — August 1983
Photographer unknown

Farm workers in the Transvaal, faces protected against a cold wind Photograph: John Seymour

Workers stacking bricks in the Eastern Cape   *Photographer unknown*

Domestic worker in Johannesburg   *Photographer unknown*

Squatter camp inside Alexandra Township, near Johannesburg   *Photographer unknown*

Single-sex hostel inside Alexandra Township — 1983   *Photograph: Nigel Dickenson*

Women's demonstration against the pass laws, Pretoria — 9 August 1956
Photographer unknown

Women resisting the issue of passbooks in Zeerust — 1957 *Photographer unknown*

Arrest under the pass laws in Johannesburg *Photographer unknown*

Suppression of women's protest in Cato Manor — 1959   Photograph: Laurie Bloomfield

Lilian Ngoyi at the head of a demonstration against the pass laws   Photograph: Eli Weinberg

At the Congress of the People, Kliptown — June 1955   Photograph: Eli Weinberg

Demonstration in support of those accused in the Treason Trial which started in 1956
Photograph: Eli Weinberg

Demonstration outside the court in which Nelson Mandela was facing trial in 1962
Photographer unknown

Winnie Mandela leaves the court after Nelson Mandela had been sentenced to prison in 1962
Photograph: Ernest Cole

Protesting against the setting up of the segregated tricameral parliament, Durban 1983
Photographer unknown

Residents of New Crossroads, near Cape Town, demonstrating against rent increases at the offices of the Western Cape Development Board — January 1985   Photographer unknown

Residents from Houtbay, near Cape Town, calling for improved services. The women, in their work clothes, are employed in the fishing industry — 1983   Photographer unknown

At a rally in Johannesburg on South African Women's Day, organised by the Federation of South African Women — 9 August 1984   *Photographer unknown*

At a rally in Rylands near Cape Town in April 1984, organised jointly by the United Women's Organisation and the Women's Front, to mark the thirtieth anniversary of the founding of the Federation of South African Women   *Photographer unknown*

References

ABBREVIATIONS

The following abbreviations are used:

Cit	*The Citizen*, Johannesburg.
CT	*Cape Times*, Cape Town.
DD	*Daily Dispatch*, East London.
Debates	*House of Assembly Debates (Hansard)*, Cape Town/Pretoria.
DN	*Daily News*, Durban.
FM	*Financial Mail*, Johannesburg.
GN	*The Guardian*, London.
Post	*Post*, Johannesburg.
RDM	*Rand Daily Mail*, Johannesburg.
SAIRR	South African Institute of Race Relations,
S	*Sowetan*, Johannesburg.
SALDRU	Southern African Labour and Development Research Unit.
S.Exp	*Sunday Express*, Johannesburg.
ST(Jbg)	*Sunday Times*, Johannesburg.
WIP	*Work in Progress*, Southern Africa Research Service, Johannesburg.

INTRODUCTION

1. *Survey of Race Relations in South Africa* South African Institute of Race Relations, Johannesburg, 1983, p.67; C Simkins, 'The distribution of the African population of South Africa by age, sex and region-type: 1960-1980', *SALDRU Working Paper*, No. 32, Cape Town, January 1981, p.3.

PART I MIGRANT LABOUR AND SEGREGATION

I.1 Migrant Labour

1. C Simkins, 'The distribution of the African population of South Africa by age, sex and region-type: 1960-1980', *SALDRU Working Paper* No. 32, South African Labour Development Research Unit, Cape Town, January 1981.
2. Spies, *Urban-Rural Interaction*, Stellenbosch, p.69.
3. Francis Wilson, *Migrant Labour in South Africa*, Johannesburg 1972.
4. *Debates*, Cape Town, 6.2.68.
5. *Debates*, Cape Town, 23.5.69.
6. *Debates*, Cape Town, 24.4.68.
7. *Star*, 30.6.73.
8. *Debates*, Cape Town, 17.3.64.
9. *Black Sash*, 1974.
10. *South African Statistics*, 1982, Department of Statistics, Pretoria, 1982.

I.2 Influx Control

11. J Yawitch, 'African Women and Labour Force Participation', *WIP*, No. 9, August 1979, p.34.

12. L Clarke & J Ngobese, *Women Without Men*, Institute for Black Research, Durban, 1975; M V Gandar & N Bromberger, 'Economic and demographic functioning of rural households: Mahlabahini District, KwaZulu', *Reality*, Pietermaritzburg, September, 1984; *S.Exp*, 4.11.84.
13. J Yawitch, *op. cit.*, p.38.
14. J Cock et al. 'Women and Changing Relations of Control', *South African Review I — Same Foundations, New Facades?*, Southern African Research Service, Johannesburg, 1983, p.282.
15. *DD*, 30.4.80.
16. J Cock et al. *op. cit.*, p.283.
17. J Cock et al. *op. cit.*, p.285.
18. *Star*, 24.10.83.
19. *Apartheid: The Facts*, IDAF, 1983, p.45; *FOCUS* No. 52, May-June 1984; *Debates* 1980-1984.

I.3 Forced Removals

20. Press Release: 'Forced Removals in South Africa — The Reports of the Surplus People Project', Cape Town, January 1983.
21. E Wait (ed.), *South Africa, a land divided*, Black Sash, Johannesburg, 1982, p.2.
22. *Ibid.*, p.2.
23. J Yawitch, *Betterment — The myth of homeland agriculture*, SAIRR, Johannesburg, 1981, p.86.
24. 'The Effects of Apartheid on the Status of Women in Southern Africa', Document submitted to the World Conference of the United Nations Decade for Women, Copenhagen, 14-30 July 1980, A/CONF 94/7, p.4.
25. 'Forced removals in South Africa 1977-1978', paper prepared by IDAF for the *United Nations Centre Against Apartheid*, No. 44/78, Oct. 1978, p.9.
26. *FM*, 29.7.84.
27. *GN*, 23.9.81.
28. J. Yawitch, 'Women and Squatting', in P Bonner (ed.) *Working Papers in Southern African Studies*, Vol. 2, Cape Town, 1981, pp.223, 224.

I.4 In the Bantustans

29. H J Simons, *African Women: their Legal Status in South Africa*, London, 1968.
30. J Cock, *Maids and Madams, A Study in the Politics of Exploitation*, Ravan Press, Johannesburg, 1980, p.310.
31. E Wait (ed.) *op. cit.*, p.32.
32. *CH*, 13.8.83.
33. H J Simons, *op. cit.*, p.187.
34. *Ibid.*, pp.187-188.
35. *Ibid.*, p.188.
36. C Kros, 'Urban African Women's Organisations 1935-1956', *Africa Perspectives Dissertation No. 3*, University of the Witwatersrand, Sept. 1980, reprinted Dec. 1982, p.13.

37. *Ibid.,* p.13.
38. P Ntantala, 'African Tragedy', *Africa South,* Vol. 1. No.3, 1957.
39. United Nations Document A/CONF 94/7, *op. cit.,* p.6.
40. H J Simons, *op. cit.,* p.264.
41. *Ibid.,* p.266.
42. J Cock, *op. cit.,* p.358; *Transkei Legislative Assembly Debates,* 1976, p.227.
43. *New African,* London, July 1981, p.18.
44. *FT,* 2.1.82.
45. *Ibid.*

PART II HEALTH, WELFARE AND THE FAMILY

II.1 Marriage and the Family

1. *DN,* 27.11.82; 7.12.83.
2. *Debates,* Cape Town, 6.3.62.
3. E S Landis, *Apartheid and the Disabilities of African Women in South Africa,* United Nations Unit on Apartheid, Dec. 1973.
4. A de Kock, 'Matrimonial Property and Women's Legal Disabilities', paper given at the 1976 National Convention to Advance Women's Legal Rights; quoted in J Cock, *Maids and Madams, a Study in the Politics of Exploitation,* Ravan Press, Johannesburg, 1980, p.243.
5. *FM,* 13.7.84; 26.10.84.
6. *RDM,* 1.11.83; *CT,* 6.6.84.
7. *WIP,* No. 27, 1983, pp.36-7.
8. *SAIRR Survey* 1982, p.289; *WIP,* No. 27, 1983, p.37.
9. *WIP,* No. 27, 1983, p.39.
10. *Ibid.,* p.37.
11. *Ibid.*
12. 'The Effects of Apartheid on the Status of Women in Southern Africa', Document submitted to the World Conference of the United Nations Decade for Women, Copenhagen, July 1980, A/CONF 94/7, p.21.
13. *RDM,* 30.6.83; 10.8.84.
14. *WIP,* No. 12, April 1980, p.51.
15. *Soweto: A Study by the Transvaal Region of the Urban Foundation,* Johannesburg, 1980; p.147.
16. *Star,* 9.10.82.
17. *WIP, op. cit.,* p.50.
18. *Ibid.,* p.52.
19. *Ibid.,* pp.53,57.
20. *RDM,* 1.8.80.
21. *RDM* 1.8.80; *Cit.* 10.3.81.
22. *Star,* 9.10.82.
23. *RDM,* 11.8.81.
24. M Wilson, 'The changing status of African women', Fifth Bertha Solomon Memorial Lecture, Port Elizabeth, 1974, reprinted in *South African Outlook,* Cape Town, January 1983, pp.11-13.
25. *Black Sash,* August 1973.
26. *WIP,* No. 27, June 1983, p.41.
27. *Ibid.*
28. *Ibid.*
29. *South African Bulletin of Statistics,* Central Statistical Services, Pretoria, 1980 and 1982.

II.2 Children

30. R Simons, 'The Developing Situation of Urban and Rural Women', Paper presented to the Conference of ANC Women, Luanda, Sept. 1981, p.11.

31. Quoted in Sheena Duncan, 'The Illegal Children', *Black Sash,* Feb. 1973.
32. United Nations Document A/CONF 94/7, *op. cit.,* p.22.
33. *WIP,* No. 27, June 1983, p.35.

II.3 Social Security

34. United Nations Document A/CONF 94/7, *op. cit.,* p.32.
35. *Ibid.,* p.32; *South African Labour Bulletin,* Johannesburg, Vol. 10, No. 1, 1984, p.35.
36. L Clarke and J Ngobese, *Women Without Men,* Institute for Black Research, Durban, 1975, p.52.
37. *CT,* 29.3.84; *RDM,* 28.6.84; United Nations Document A/CONF 94/7, *op. cit.,* pp.32 & 33.
38. Y S Meer and M D Mlaba, *Apartheid — our picture,* Institute for Black Research, Durban, 1982, p.117.
39. J Cock *et al.* 'Women and Changing Relations of Control', *South African Review I — Same Foundations, New Facades?,* South African Research Service, Johannesburg 1983, p.278.

II.4 Control of Fertility — or Populations

40. Quoted in M Gray, 'Race Ratios: The Politics of Population Control in South Africa', L Bordestam and S Bergstrom (ed.) *Poverty and Population Control,* London, 1980, p.147.
41. *Ibid..*
42. *GN,* 14.4.83.
43. Quoted in *Anti-Apartheid Women's Committee Newsletter,* London, No. 1, Nov-Dec 1981.
44. *RDM,* 20.1.82.
45. 'Family Planning in South Africa — A kind of genocide?', *The African Communist,* London, No. 90, 1982, p.76.
46. *Ibid.,* p.79.
47. 'Women and Apartheid', *Objective: Justice,* United Nations Department of Public Information, Vol. XII, No. 1, August 1980, p.34.
48. B Klugman, 'The Political Economy of Population Control in South Africa', BA Dissertation, University of the Witwatersrand, Feb. 1980, p.72.
49. 'Cancer of the Cervix', *Critical Health,* No. 9, May 1983, p.71.
50. B Klugman, *op. cit.,* p.73.
51. *Ibid.,* p.73.
52. *Anti-Apartheid Women's Committee Newsletter, op. cit.*
53. *The African Communist, op. cit.*
54. J Cock, *Maids and Madams, A Study in the Politics of Exploitation,* Ravan Press, Johannesburg, 1980, p.259.
55. *RDM,* 1.10.76; J Cock, *op. cit.,* p.260.
56. J Cock, *op cit.,* p.260; *RDM,* 1.10.76.
57. *The African Communist, op. cit.*
58. *RDM,* 1.10.76.
59. J Cock, *op. cit.,* p.260.
60. *S. Exp.* 9.8.81.

II.5 Rape

61. *S. Exp.* 4.10.81.
62. *CT,* 9.3.78.
63. J Cock, *op. cit.,* p.261.

64. *S. Exp.* 1.8.82.
65. J Cock, 'Women and Health', *NUSAS Conference on Women*, Paper delivered at first NUSAS Conference on Women held at the University of the Witwatersrand, July 1982, NUSAS Women's Directive, Cape Town, 1983.
66. *CT,* 9.3.78, quoted in *From Women,* Cape Town, No. 11, June 1978, p.3.
67. *From Women, op. cit.*
68. J Cock, *op. cit.,* p.261.
69. *From Women, op. cit.*
70. *S. Exp.* 4.10.81.
71. *RDM,* 30.10.82.

II.6 Health and Poverty in the Countryside

72. Medical Officer of Health Reports; *Survey of Race Relations,* South African Institute of Race Relations, 1982, p.528. Table in A Seedat, *Crippling a Nation — Health in Apartheid South Africa,* IDAF, London, 1984, p.26.
73. *Demographic Yearbook, 1980,* information provided by Office of Population Censuses and Surveys, London, December 1983; in *A Seedat, op. cit.,* p.27.
74. United Nations Document A/CONF 94/7, *op. cit.,* p.35.
75. *Critical Health,* No. 9, May 1983, 'Women and Health', pp.436-9.
76. United Nations Document A/CONF 94/7, *op. cit.,* p.34.
77. L Bordestam & S Bergstrom (ed.) *op. cit.,* p.152.
78. J Yawitch, 'Natal 1959 — The Women's Protests', Development Studies Group (ed.) *Collected Papers of the Conference on the History of Opposition in Southern Africa,* University of the Witwatersrand, Jan. 1978, p.4.
79. United Nations Document A/CONF 94/7, *op. cit.,* p.34.
80. *GN,* 14.4.83.
81. *DN,* 13.4.83.
82. *GN,* 14.4.83.
83. Black Sash Yellow Sheet No. 19, Johannesburg, March 1981, p.4.
84. *Ibid.*
85. *Ibid.,* p.35.
86. *Ibid.*
87. *Resettlement,* Conference Papers, 51st Annual Council Meeting, South African Institute of Race Relations, Johannesburg, 1981, p.60.
88. *Ibid.,* p.50.

PART III AT WORK

III.1 Overview

1. *Bulletin of Statistics,* Central Statistical Services, Pretoria, September 1983, Table 2.1.
2. *Ibid.*
3. *Population Census 80: Economic Characteristics,* Central Statistical Services, Pretoria, 1980.
4. *Ibid.*
5. *Ibid.*
6. J Cock et al. *op. cit.,* p.286.
7. 'The Effects of Apartheid on the Status of Women in Southern Africa', Document submitted to the World Conference of the United Nations Decade for Women, Copenhagen, July 1980, A/CONF 94/7, p.27.

8. *Focus on Political Repression in Southern Africa,* 45, March-April 1983, p.1; 52, May-June 1984, p.7, IDAF, London.
9. R Lapchick & S Urdang, 'The effects of apartheid on the employment of women in South Africa, and a history of the role of women in the trade unions', Background paper for the World Conference of the United Nations Decade for Women, Copenhagen, July 1980, A/CONF 94/BP/16, p.3.
10. *Ibid.*
11. J Yawitch, 'African Women and Labour-Force Participation', *WIP,* No. 9, August 1979, p.39.

III.2 Agriculture

12. R Lapchick & S Urdang, *op. cit.,* p.17.
13. *Die Burger* 2.2.83.
14. R Lapchick & S Urdang, *op. cit.,* p.17.
15. *Ibid.,* p.18.
16. *Ibid; Star,* 10.9.81, 2.3.84; *Submission to Manpower Commission on Farm Labour,* Farm Labour Project, Johannesburg, 1982, p.11.
17. Farm Labour Project, *op. cit.,* p.14.

III.3 Domestic Workers

18. *Population Census 80, op. cit.*
19. J Cock, *op. cit.*
20. R Lapchick & S Urdang, *op. cit.,* p.11; *CH,* 5.5.84; *S,* 19.6.84.
21. J Cock, *op. cit.,* p.45.
22. *Ibid.,* p.46.
23. *Ibid.,* p.47.
24. *Ibid.,* p.49.
25. *Ibid.,* p.54.
26. *Ibid.,* p.262.
27. *Ibid.,* p.263.
28. *Ibid.,* pp.113,114.
29. *Ibid.,* p. 116.
30. *Workers Unity,* London, No. 25, April 1981, p.7.

III.4 Manufacturing Industry

31. J Lewis, 'Solly Sachs and the Garment Workers Union', *Essays in South African Labour History,* ed. E Webster, Ravan Press, Johannesburg, 1978, p.189.
32. A Mullins, 'Working women speak', in *WIP,* No. 27, June 1983, p.38.
33. *Grassroots,* July/August 1982.
34. J Yawitch, 1979, *op. cit.,* p.42; J Cock *et al,* 'Women and Changing Relations of Control', *op. cit.,* pp.279,285.
35. *Ibid,* p.285.
36. R Lapchick & S Urdang, *op. cit.,* p.19.
37. J Cock, *et al, op. cit.,* pp.293-294.
38. *Grassroots,* March 1984.
39. *Africa Perspective,* July 1979, p.34.
40. *Critical Health,* Johannesburg, No. 9, 1983, p.27. 41. *Voice,* Johannesburg, 20.5.78.

III.5 Border Industries

41. *House of Assembly Debates,* 29.5.65.
42. R Lapchick & S Urdang, *op. cit.,* p.22.

43. *Grassroots*, Cape Town, 1981.
44. Ethel Wait (ed.) *South Africa, a land divided*, Black Sash, Johannesburg, 1982, p.17.

III.6 The Informal Sector

45. *Annual Survey of Race Relations*, SAIRR, 1983, p.278.
46. *CT*, 1.4.82.
47. A Brooks & J Brickhill, *Whirlwind Before the Storm*, IDAF, London, 1980, Part VI.
48. *SASPU National*, Vol. 1, No. 4, November 1980, p.10.

III.7 Professions

49. *Population Census 80, op. cit.*
50. *South Africa 1984. Official Yearbook of the Republic of South Africa*, Chris van Rensburg Publications, Johannesburg, 1984, p.707.
51. F Troup, *Forbidden Pastures: Education under Apartheid*, IDAF, London, 1976, p.40.
52. *Star*, 30.1.84; *DD*, 12.4.84.
53. R Lapchick & S Urdang, *op. cit.*, p.27; A Seedat, *op. cit.*, p. 92.
54. R Lapchick & S Urdang, *op. cit.*, p.28.
55. A Seedat, *Crippling a Nation – Health In Apartheid South Africa*, IDAF, London 1983, p.92.
56. *South African Statistics 1982*, Department of Statistics, Pretoria, 1982, p.126.
57. *Population Census 80, op. cit.*
58. *Christian Science Monitor*, 20.10.82.

III.8 Trends and Patterns of Discrimination

59. *Current Population Survey: Blacks and Coloureds 1979-81*,Report No. 07-07-01, Department of Statistics, Pretoria, 1982.
60. J Cock et al. *op. cit.*, p.285.
61. National Manpower Surveys, Department of Manpower Utilisation, Pretoria, 1973-81; Table in J Cock et al. *Op. cit.*, p.287.
62. *Star*, 1.5.76.
63. *Manpower Survey No. 15, 29 April 1983*, Occupations according to Sector Groups, Department of Manpower, Pretoria, 1984.
64. *Christian Science Monitor*, 20.10.82.
65. *Ibid.*
66. *ST (Jbg)*, 28.10.79.
67. F Troup, *op. cit.*
68. J Cock, *op. cit.*, p.266.
69. *Ibid.*, p.276.
70. *Ibid.*, p.277.
71. *Population Census 80:* Sample Tabulation — Social Charactistics Report No. 02-80-02, Central Statistical Services, Pretoria, 1982. *(These figures exclude people in the bantustans of Transkei, Bophuthatswana and Venda.)*

III.9 Trade Unions

72. R Lapchick & S Urdang, *op. cit.*, p.23.
73. *Directory of South African Trade Unions*, Southern Africa Labour & Development Research Unit, Cape Town, 1984.

PART IV POLITICAL STRUGGLE

IV.1 History of Struggle

1. 'The Role of Women in the Struggle for Liberation in Zimbabwe, Namibia and South Africa', Document submitted to the World Conference of the United Nations Decade for Women, Copenhagen, July 1980, A/CONF 94/5, p.12.
2. C Walker, *Women and Resistance in South Africa*, Onyx Press, London, 1982.
3. F Meer (ed.) *Black Woman*, University of Natal, Durban, 1975.
4. *Ibid.*
5. C Walker, *op. cit.*, p.110.
6. *Ibid.*, p.109.

IV.2 Women's Resistance

7. S Plaatje, *Native Life in South Africa*, Penguin, 1969,
8. C Walker, *op. cit.*
9. M Benson, *Struggle for a Birthright*, Penguin, 1966,
10. J Yawitch, 'Natal 1959 — The Women's Protests', Paper presented at the Conference on the History of Opposition in South Africa, University of the Witwatersrand, Jan. 1978, p.214.
11. J Yawitch, 1978, *op. cit.*, p.214; 'The Role of Women in the Struggle for Liberation in Zimbabwe, Namibia and South Africa', Document submitted to the World Conference of the United Nations Decade for Women, Copenhagen, July 1980, A/CONF 94/5, p.19.5.
12. C Hooper, *Brief Authority*, London, 1960.
13. *Ibid.*
14. J Yawitch, 1978, *op. cit.*, p.220.
15. *Ibid.*
16. *Ibid.*, p.218.
17. *Ibid.*, p.220.

IV.4 Legacy of Hope and Defiance

18. C Walker, *op. cit.*, p.217.
19. *Ibid.*
20. Winnie Mandela in a speech to Soweto residents in June 1976.
21. United Nations Document A/CONF 94/5, *op. cit.*, p.23.
22. C Walker, *op. cit.*, pp.276, 278.
23. United Nations Document A/CONF 94/5, *op. cit.*, p.24.
24. *Focus on Political Repression in Southern Africa*, No. 53, p.1. IDAF, London.
25. *Ibid., RDM*, 21.8.84.

IV.6 Soweto and After

26. United Nations Document A/CONF 94/5, *op. cit.*, p.26.
27. *Ibid.*, p.27.
28. *Social Review*, Cape Town, Nov. 1981, p.23.
29. *S*, 10.2.84, 9.3.84; *Star*, 3.8.84.
30. *CT*, 24.10.80.
31. *RDM*, 22.9.80.
32. *Beyond Reform: the challenge of change*, Speeches prepared at the NUSAS July Festival held at the University of Cape Town, July 1983; *WIP* No. 21, February 1982; *WIP* No. 34, 1984.

33. *WIP*, No. 34, 1984; *SASPU National,* December 1984.

34. *Grassroots,* Cape Town, March 1983.

35. *WIP*, No. 34, 1984; *Solidarity News Service,* Gaberones, 17.8.84.

36. *CT*, 3.8.84; 14.8.84.

37. *Post,* 8.10.80.

38. *The Sun Will Rise,* 16mm film, IDAF, London 1982.

39. *Star,* 6.12.83.

V LOOKING FORWARD

1. J Cock, *Maids and Madams, A Study in the Politics of Exploitation,* Ravan Press, Johannesburg, 1980, p.312.

2. *Voice of Women,* Special Conference Issue, ANC, Lusaka, 1981.

3. J Yawitch, 'Women and Squatting, a Winterveld Case Study', in P. Bonner (ed.), *Working Papers in Southern African Studies, Vol. 2,* Cape Town, 1981, p.224.

Index

Abortion 51-2, 70.
Administration Boards (*now* Development Boards) 127.
African National Congress (ANC) 83, 84, 85, 86, 97, 98, 104, 110.
Women's League (ANCWL) 86, 96-7, 104, 110, 111, 116.
agriculture 59-60, 114.
in bantustans 9, 16, 30.
alcoholism 45.
Alexander, Ray 79.
ANC *see* African National Congress.
apartheid system 7-11, 12, 13, 15, 48, 114-15, 124-7.
Asian (term), defined 125.
assault and torture 98-102, 104.

Baard, Frances 79.
bans and banishment 79, 84, 85, 92, 99, 104, 105, 111-13.
Bantu Women's League 86.
bantustans 8-9, 12, 27-34, 93, 125, 126.
border industries 32, 69, 70-1, 127.
closer settlements 39, 126.
employment 32.
health 54, 56-7.
as a labour source 32, 114.
land allocation 8, 30-1.
movement from 20.
resettlement camps/areas 22, 31, 34, 56, 126.
beer and beerhalls 72, 93, 95-6.
birth control *see* contraception.
Black (term), defined 125.
black consciousness movement 105.
Black Sash 82, 88, 106-7.
Black Spots 126.
Black Women Unite 106, 108.
Black Women's Federation (BWF) 103, 104, 105.
Bophuthatswana bantustan 22, 33-4.
boycotts 84, 94-6, 106.
BWF *see* Black Women's Federation.

Children:
diseases 50, 56.
infant mortality 48-9, 53-4, 55, 56, Table V.
and marriage break-up 35, 36.
and parental imprisonment 20, 99, 102.
pregnancy among school-students 77.
residence rights 40, 42-3, 45-6.
right to have 69-70.
Churches:
Dutch Reformed Church (DRC): and migrant labour system, its effect on family life 15.
and population control 48.
South African Council of Churches 67, 103.
Ciskei bantustan 33.
relocation camps in 22.
citizenship, denial of 14.
colonialism 7, 9, 29, 35.

Coloured (term), defined 125.
Coloured women 58, 60, 74, 75, 76.
Communist Party 83.
community groups 23.
'commuters' 13, 19, 127, Table II.
Congress movement 83, 88-9, 95.
see also under names of organisations
constitutional changes (1984) 114.
opposition to 109.
contraception 48-51.
Crossroads 24, 25.

Death penalty 53, 111.
de Beer, Dr J, *quoted* 49.
Defiance Campaign 83-4.
dependency 16-17, 18, 22-3, 31, 37, 66, 68.
detention 84, 85, 98, 99, 103-4, 105.
Development Boards (*formerly* Administration Boards) 127.
Dipale, Ernest 101.
Dipale, Joyce 100.
discrimination 7, 10-11, 59, 67, 69, 75-6.
diseases *see under* health.
Dlamini, Nkosazana, *quoted* 103.
Domestic Workers and Employers Project (DWEP) 67.
Domestic Workers Project (DWP) 67.
du Toit, Bettie 79; *quoted* 78.

Education 73-4, 76-7.
Bantu, campaigns against 95, 102-4.
schools (unregistered) 95.
vocational training 73, 76.
Eiselen, Dr. W. M., *quoted* 90-1, 93.
employment:
in bantustans 32.
conditions 61-2, 63-4, 69-70, 73-4.
exclusion from 8-9, 16, 32.
figures 58-9, 68-9, 73, 75, 76.
holidays 63.
legal qualifications 40-1, 60, 127.
legislation, lack of 61, 63.
strikes 79.
workers organisations 67.
workforce: composition of Tables VII, VIII, IX.
increase in 20, 75, Table VI.
see also wages.
categories: agriculture 30, 58, 59-62, 75, 76, 114.
domestic 16, 58, 59, 62-5, 66-7, 76.
'illegals' 19-20, 59, 72, 128.
informal sector 58, 71-2.
manufacturing 58, 68-70, 75.
professions 58, 73-5, 76.
service industries 58, 69, 75-6.
see also 'commuters'; migrant labour system.
equal rights *see* legal rights.
exploitation 62-5, 71.

Family life 38-45, 64, 117.
  housing restrictions and 13.
  migrant labour system and 9, 13-16, 18, 38, 67.
  see also Black Sash; squatters.
Federation of South African Women (FSAW) (later
  FEDSAW) 83, 86-7, 88, 97, 98, 101, 104, 106, 108, 110,
  111.
First, Ruth 110.
Free Mandela Campaign 106.
Freedom Charter 84.
Freedom Day 84.
Froneman, G F van L, quoted 14.
FSAW see Federation of South African Women.

Gazankulu bantustan 33.
Goonam, Dr 83.
Graser, Roland 52.
Grobbelaar, Arthur, quoted 50.
Group Areas Policy 125-6.
Gumede, Elizabeth 101.

Health:
  in bantustans 50, 54, 56-7.
  charges 54.
  diseases 50, 54-6, 75.
  education 49-50.
  expenditure 50.
  maternity care/leave 54, 69-70.
  see also contraception; mental health.
Hogan, Barbara 102.
Homelands see bantustans.
housing and accommodation 9, 13, 18, 19, 24, 39-40, 41,
  94.
  hostels 41-3, 71, 125.
  see also squatters.
hunger strikes 101.

Identity Documents see passes.
'illegals' 19-20, 59, 71, 72, 128.
Indian women 75, 76, 82, 83.
infant mortality see under children.
influx control see pass laws/influx control.

Joseph, Helen 87, 89.
  quoted 97, 98.

Keagile, Lilian 101.
Khali, Sally 107.
Khayelitsha 25.
Kotze, Coen, quoted 46.
KwaZulu bantustan 36.

Labour Bureaux 18, 32, 41, 60, 127.
labour system see employment; migrant labour system.
land 16, 39, 60, 83.
  allocation 8, 29-30, 31, 124.
  'consolidation' 126.
  dispossession 8.
  hunger 30-2.
legal rights 28-9, 31-2, 33, 35-8, 40-1, 105.
legislation 84, 98.
  Abortion and Sterilisation Act (1975) 51.
  Asiatic Land Tenure and Representation Act 83.
  Bantu Authorities Act 90.
  Blacks (Urban Areas) Act (Section 10) 128;
    (Section 29) 41.
  Industrial Conciliation Act 63, 69, 78, 79.

Internal Security Act 102.
  Labour Relations Act 63, 69.
  Matrimonial Affairs Act (1953) 37.
  Matrimonial Property Act (1984) 37.
  Nursing Act (1957) 73.
  Suppression of Communism Act (1950) 79.
  Trespass Act 39.
  Unemployment Insurance Act 63.
  Wages Act 63, 69.
  Workmen's Compensation Act 63.
liberation struggle see resistance and liberation struggle.
lobolo 35-6.
Luckett, Kathy, quoted 26.
Lutuli, Albert, quoted 98.

Mafekeng, Elizabeth 79.
Mahlangu, Martha 111.
Mahlangu, Solomon 111.
Makhoere, Caesarina 101.
Malestoe, Makgoro 91.
malnutrition 50, 54-6.
Manana, Mrs quoted 111.
Manana, Naphtali 111.
Mandela, Nelson 106, 112.
Mandela, Winnie 103, 112.
marriage 44-5, 64, Table III.
  and land allocation 31.
  laws 35-8.
  migrant labour system and 13, 15-16, 30, 38.
  removals/relocation and 23.
  residence rights and 41.
  see also family life; squatters.
Maxeke, Charlotte 86.
Mbatha, Khosi 99, 100.
Meer, Dr Fatima 103, 105, 113.
  quoted 82.
mental health 54, 56-7.
migrant labour system 8-9, 12-16, 18, 38, 42, 60, 67, 114,
  117, 127.
  figures 58-9, Table II.
  'illegals' 59, 71, 128.
  mental health and 57.
  see also squatters.
Mji, Sikose, quoted 103.
Mkhize, Florence 110.
Mncadi, Dr Margaret 93.
Modise, Thandi 99, 104.
Moodley, Mary 79.
Morrison, George, quoted 25.
Mosololi, Jerry 111.
Mosololi, Sarah, quoted 111.
Motlana, Dr Nthato, quoted 50.
Motlana, Sally 103.
Mtintso, Thenjwe 104.

Naidoo, Shanthie 100-1.
Natal Code 35, 36.
Natal Organisation of Women 106.
National Forum 108.
Ncapai, Greta 111.
Ndzanga, Rita 99-100.
Ngoyi, Lilian 65, 87, 89.
  quoted 88, 113.
Ninzi, Lucy, quoted 106.
Ntsatha, Jane 99.
Ntwana, Ida 87.

135

Nyembe, Dorothy 101.
Nzima, Jabu 110.

Oppenheimer, Mrs Harry 107.
organisations 67, 78, 81-8 *passim*, 103-9.
  self-help associations 104.
  see also under individual names.

Pan-Africanist Congress (PAC) 84, 85, 97.
pass laws/influx control 8-9, 10, 12, 16-20, 32, 38, 39, 44,
  127, 128.
  arrests, figures Table IV.
  Endorsed Out 128.
  'illegals' 19-20, 59, 71, 128.
  see also migrant labour system; squatters.
passes (Pass Book) 12, 17, 78-9, 127.
  protests/resistance 17-18, 84, 85-6, 87-93, 96-8,
  110-11.
pensions and allowances 47-8, 69.
Pityana, Dimza 103.
police brutality 24-5, 26, 53, 83, 84, 91, 95, 96, 102-4,
  107.
  see also assault and torture.
population control 9, 48-9.
population figures Table I.
Pretorius, Connie 76.
prison conditions 20, 98, 99-102.
property ownership *see* legal rights.

Ramphele, Dr Mamphela 103, 104, 112.
rape 23, 52-3.
reference book *see* passes.
removals/relocation 9-10, 12, 13, 14-15, 21-4, 30-1, 38,
  39, 55, 60, 126-7.
  camps/areas 22, 30-1, 34, 56.
  health and 55, 56, 57.
  resistance to 24-6.
residence rights 12, 14, 18-19, 40, 41, 46, 127.
  of children 40, 42, 45-6.
resistance and liberation struggle 81-3, 85-93, 98-9,
  108-9.
  armed struggle 85, 104.
  to Bantu education 95, 102-4.
  Defiance Campaign 83-4.
  historical overview 81-5.
  to hostel life 42-3.
  to pass laws 17-18, 84, 85-6, 87-93, 96-8, 110-11.
  passive resistance 25, 82, 83-5, 104.
  refugees from 91-2.
  to removals 24-6.
  repressive response to 23, 24-6, 79, 84-5, 91, 95, 96,
  98-102, 103-4, 109-10.
  trade unions and 78-80.
  and women's liberation 11, 81, 116-17.
  see also boycotts; squatters.
Riekert Commission 19.

SADWA *see* South African Domestic Workers
  Association.
Schoon, Jeanette and Katryn 110.
Seroke, Joyce 103.
Serokolo, Montshidisi 99.
Sharpeville massacre (1960) 84, 97, 104.
Silinga, Annie 110-11.
Simons, Ray 87.
Sisulu, Albertina Nontsikelelo and family 111-12.
social security 46-8.

South African Domestic Workers Association
  (SADWA) 67.
South African Indian Congress 83.
South African Institute of Race Relations 67.
Soweto 45, 95.
  hostel accommodation 42.
  housing shortage 39, 40.
  uprising (1976) 102-3, 107.
  squatters 13, 20, 21, 22, 24-6, 38, 40, 94-5, 126.
status and self-image 27, 35, 43-4, 64, 66-7, 77, 115.
sterilisation 49, 70.
strikes 79, 82, 85.
subordination 9, 17, 28-9, 35-8, 62, 77, 82.

Tamana, Dora, *quoted* 110.
Tambo, Oliver, *quoted* 116.
Tema, Sophie 103.
Theoabale, Mpho 104.
torture and assault 98-102, 104.
townships 12-13, 19, 21, 40, 70, 94-5, 96, 125, 126-7.
  hostel accommodation 41-3, 125.
  quality of life 45.
  rape 69.
  see also Soweto.
trade unions and unionists 67, 78-80, 87, 100, 108.
Transkei bantustan 24, 25-30, 33.
Troskie, Dr Chris, *quoted* 49.

UDF *see* United Democratic Front.
unemployment 20, 41, 59, 68, 70, 71.
  see also social security.
United Democratic Front (UDF) 100, 108, 109, 111, 112.
United Women's Organisation (UWO) 105-6, 108, 109,
  110.

Valiamma 82.
van der Merwe, Dr Nak 48-9, 55.
van Rensburg, Dr N J 49.
Venda bantustan 33.
Verwoerd, Dr, *quoted* 70, 73, 77.
Viljoen Commission 39.
violence 23, 45, 52-3.
Vorster, B J, *quoted* 14.
voting rights 10, 83.

Wages and incomes 9, 17, 61, 63, 68, 70-1, 73, 76.
water supplies 22, 25, 56.
Weinberg, Sheila 113.
white women 10-11.
  abortion figures 51.
  birth control, attitudes re 48, 49-50.
  civil defence training 66.
  education and training 73.
  employment 60, 69, 74, 75.
  life style 65-6.
  marriage figures 45, Table III.
  organisations 82-3, 106-8.
  and resistance/liberation struggle 82-3, 88, 94, 95,
  107-8.
  and trade union movement 78.
  voting rights 11, 83.
Women for Peace 107.
Women's Charter 87.
Women's Day 88, 106, 109.
women's liberation 11, 27, 81, 116-17.

Zihlangu, Dorothy, *quoted* 89.

136